ARMSTRONGISM'S

300 ERRORS

EXPOSED

ARMSTRONGISM'S
300 ERRORS
EXPOSED

BY 1300 BIBLE VERSES

Stanley E. Anderson

BAKER BOOK HOUSE
Grand Rapids, Michigan

ARMSTRONGISM'S 300 ERRORS EXPOSED
by 1300 Bible Verses
Stanley E. Anderson, Th.D.
1300 Tyler Lane, Elgin, Ill.

Reprinted 1975
by Baker Book House
ISBN: 0-8010-0089-0

Library of Congress Card Catalog Number 77-185796

Printed in the United States of America

PREFACE

"BELOVED, WHEN I gave all diligence to write unto you of the common salvation, it was needful for me to write unto you, and exhort you that ye should earnestly contend for the faith which was once delivered unto the saints. For there are certain men crept in unawares . . ." (Jude 3, 4).

Of the 27 Books of the New Testament, 26 of them warn us against heresies. Each Christian, then, is commanded—not merely advised—to contend for the faith and against "certain men" who try desperately to creep into our homes via radio, television and mail.

"But I don't like to argue or to be negative," some will say. Nor does anyone like to see his neighbor's house burn down, but if fire starts he will fight it most earnestly. He knows the next house to burn may be his own. A "permissive" neighbor may not want to bother with dandelions and other weeds in his lawn or garden, but those weeds spread.

And how lenient should we be with dope pushers? They tempt our teenagers and adults who, if addicted, turn to crime for funds. From 50 to 80 per cent of the crime that makes our cities unlivable, says *Newsweek*, is due to drugs.

Many of America's 130,000,000 Christians feel that Armstrongism is as dangerous to our churches as drugs are to a peaceful society.

For rapid growth, Armstrongism rivals Mohammedanism in its

earlier years. In attacking Christian churches, Armstrong's psychological skills rival those of the communists.

In dealing with Armstrongism we shall try to be fair, concise, and thorough. A critical approach is as needful and unavoidable as that of a fire department or a gardener. The commandments in the Bible are mostly negative. Some repetition is to be expected and it should be helpful.

This book exposes a mixed-up cult; it is not an attack on individuals.

When Christ faced His hateful foes in Matthew 23, He was stern and blunt. Paul was equally frank when exposing apostates in Second Timothy and in 11 other of his letters. Peter was rough with false prophets in his second epistle; John warned us of antichrists in his three letters, and Jude defended our faith stoutly.

Frankly, we shall try to identify, explain, and refute the hundreds of fallacies in Armstrongism. But we are not infallible; we may miss some of the many published errors. Readers are invited to inform us of such—and to correct us if mistakes are found. But the Armstrong writers do not admit their most obvious blunders. Careful readers have written to them but they pose as almost immune from error.

We pray that this book will help everyone, and antagonize no one. May the Lord Jesus who "loved the church and gave Himself for it" also keep our churches safe from Armstrong's constant attacks upon them. Peter warns us about false teachers "who secretly shall bring in destructive heresies . . . with feigned words, making merchandise of you" (2 Peter 2:1, 3).

In contrast to Armstrong's dictatorial legalism, let us rejoice in Paul's salutation to his readers in 13 epistles: "*Grace* be unto you, and peace, from God our Father, and from the Lord Jesus Christ."

S. E. Anderson
Elgin, Illinois

OTHER BOOKS BY
STANLEY E. ANDERSON, TH.D.

Every Pastor A Counselor

Nehemiah The Executive

Our Dependable Bible

Your Baptism Is Important

The First Baptist

The First Church

The First Communion

Baptists Unshackled

CONTENTS

PREFACE v

1. A MUSHROOMING MOVEMENT 11

2. A CUNNING SALESMAN'S PSYCHOLOGY 17

3. COMPETING CULTS AND THEIR HIGH COSTS 22

4. DOES THE BIBLE SUPPORT ARMSTRONGISM? 31

5. GOD'S SUPREME COURT REJECTS ARMSTRONGISM 40

6. WHAT'S THE "HANDWRITING OF ORDINANCES?" 48

7. THE NEW TESTAMENT TEACHING ON LAW AND GRACE ... 51

8. REASONS FOR HONORING SUNDAY OVER SABBATH 55

9. THE PLAIN TRUTH ABOUT EASTER 66

10. ARMSTRONG DENIES FRIDAY CRUCIFIXION 71

11. THE UNITED STATES AND BRITISH COMMONWEALTH IN
    PROPHECY 75

12. A DIFFERENT PERSPECTIVE 92

13. BEWARE OF FOLLOWING STRANGERS! 95

14. ARMSTRONG'S INCREDIBLE "CHURCH" 99

15. ARMSTRONG'S "TRUE" GOSPEL 104

16. WHY WERE YOU BORN? 108

17. ARE YOU A FETUS? OR BORN AGAIN! 111

18. FALSE CONVERSION—A MORTAL DANGER 116

19. MY LETTER TO GARNER TED ARMSTRONG 119

20. IS SALVATION POSSIBLE AFTER DEATH 123

21. ARMSTRONG'S BAPTISM EXAMINED 127

22. SHOULD YOU JOIN A CHURCH? 130

23. ARMSTRONG'S CONFUSING COMMUNION 133

24. BY THEIR FRUITS YE SHALL KNOW THEM 136

25. THE HOLY SPIRIT IS A PERSON 142

26. HOW YOU CAN BE IMBUED WITH THE POWER OF GOD 147

27. WHAT DO YOU MEAN .... KINGDOM OF GOD? 150

28. ARMSTRONG FLIRTS WITH THE UNPARDONABLE SIN 153

29. PREDESTINATION: THE BIBLE VS. ARMSTRONG 156

30. IF YOU DIE, WILL YOU LIVE AGAIN? 159

31. ARE SOULS CONSCIOUS BETWEEN DEATH AND
    RESURRECTION? 162

32. LAZARUS AND THE RICH MAN REVISED 170

33. ENOCH AND ELIJAH DIES, SAYS ARMSTRONG 174

34. GARNER TED ARMSTRONG CHALLENGES GOD! 177

35. ARMSTRONGITES WANT TO BECOME GODS! 179

36. BIRTHDAY—ANOTHER ARMSTRONG TABOO 183

37. LETTERS AND MISCELLANY 186

38. I "CRASH" TWO ARMSTRONG MEETINGS 197

39. FREE FROM THE LAW! HALLELUJAH! 201

40. HOW TO DEFEAT ARMSTRONGISM 205

1

A MUSHROOMING MOVEMENT

Mr. Herbert W. Armstrong of Pasadena, California, has reason to gloat over his present worldwide empire. He calls it "The Worldwide Church of God." Like mushrooms that "spread, grow, or develop quickly," his works are also like fungus growths in that many are deadly poison.

Not many pastors, and still fewer laymen, will analyze Armstrongism in order to detect what is gospel in it and what is poison.

One of Armstrong's magazines, *The Plain Truth*, has a circulation of over 2,500,000 which could mean up to 6,000,000 readers. This number is double that of two years ago. It may double again, soon.

In January of 1973 Armstrong reported the use of about 75 television stations in the United States and Canada. And he was on about 255 radio stations, some of them in foreign countries. He boasts of "reaching, worldwide, between 150 and 200 million people" (in his 4-12-71 letter to his "Dear Brethren in God's Church," written from Jerusalem). He asserts that his work is "exerting tremendous impact on more than 150 million people around the world."

In his literature and broadcasts, Armstrong urges people to write in to his headquarters for more information. He gets results; about 2,000,000 letters come in each year. He employs a huge letter-answering staff composed of his ordained ministers

11

and graduate students. These skilled people know how to lead inquirers on and on, deeper and farther into their "one true church." One of his churches may be in your area.

Mr. Armstrong boasts that his "work" is growing at the rate of 30% each year. His gross income for 1970 was estimated at about $35,000,000; in 1972 about $55,000,000. With this vast sum he pays for his voluminous literature, his TV and radio programs, his reporters and writers worldwide, his camps and colleges, and his army of trained ministers who indoctrinate inquirers.

He maintains three colleges for training the personnel in his rapidly growing empire. His graduates, some with post-graduate degrees, then go out everywhere leading unsuspecting inquirers into their system. When sufficiently persuaded, his converts are immersed by Armstrong's agents and then are assimilated into their local congregations which are allowed to meet only if an authorized minister is present. These meetings are closed to outsiders, and only Armstrong's ministers are allowed to invite non-members to attend them.

We do not commend Armstrongism, except for its worldly efficiency. We do feel that pastors and laymen need to know enough facts about this cult so as to be warned against it.

Since two-thirds of Armstrong's converts come from our older churches, as proselytes, this means a serious leakage to this new cult. Other sects such as Mormons, Jehovah's Witnesses, Seventh-Day Adventists, and British-Israelites are constantly alert to capture our straying members.

A cult is a group of people who accept one leader, who follow him in spite of 19 centuries of Biblical teachings, who reject the mainstream of Christianity, who feel themselves to be the only chosen people, who have closed minds with antagonism toward most Christian leaders, and who are both isolationists and propagandists.

The Armstrong agents deny proselyting. They insist that they do not ask anyone for permission to visit; each prospect must ask an agent to come. Yet their printed material and their radio programs continue urging people to write in for "free" literature, and this in turn begs readers to write in requesting a minister to visit. This plan is only one of many clever psychological schemes worked out by H. W. Armstrong in his 60 years of developing salesmanship. His schemes are succeeding.

* * *

Herbert W. Armstrong was born in Des Moines, Iowa, on July 31, 1892. His father shifted from one job to another, moving his family six times before Herbert was 12. His parents were of Quaker stock, and he insists he can trace his ancestry to Edward I of England, and to a "King Herremon of Ireland" who married a daughter of Zedekiah, King of Judah. From there, the Bible carries his genealogy back to Adam! (Our chapter XI will show that this "King Herremon" is Irish folk lore, and not real history.)

I have read Mr. Armstrong's 510-page autobiography, which is only the first of a projected three-volume series. He wrote this, he said, so that he would become "visible" to his listeners and readers. And he wanted to show how he discovered "the one true church" and how all others are wrong.

It seems that young Armstrong (HWA) was bright enough in school, that he read widely and showed real ability, yet he did not finish high school. At 18, he began selling advertising for a Des Moines, Iowa, newspaper, the *Daily Capital*. In those days, he wrote of himself, he was "snappy, confident, and conceited" but not dishonest. He was "a glib talker." His salary grew from six dollars per week to eight.

Shifting jobs, he next worked for a lumber mill in Wiggins, Mississippi. Next, he worked for the *Merchants Trade Journal* in Des Moines, and there he sharpened his psychological tools for more effective advertising. He claims that the ads he wrote between his age of 20 and 23 always "got results." But here he digressed in his story; he says the most important work on earth today is the fulfillment of Matthew 24:14—"And this gospel of the kingdom shall be preached in all the world for a witness unto all nations; and then shall the end come."

This verse, says HWA, "is the only true gospel" but he is squarely contradicted by Paul (1 Cor. 15:1-4). HWA refers to Mark 13:10 where he mistakenly assumes the word "published" (King James Version) to mean printed publications! (Printing in the western world began in 1456.) The word "published" in

Mark 13:10 is the same Greek word as "preached" in Matthew 24:14. It is *kerusso,* used 61 times in the New Testament.

HWA shows some pride in his wide reading. But he could have learned much from the Ethiopian official in Acts 8:26-40. Our Lord instructed Philip, the deacon and evangelist, to meet this Ethiopian and ask him if he understood what he was reading in the scroll of Isaiah. "How can I," he said, "except some man should guide me?" Then he asked Philip for help. Apparently, HWA did not follow similar divine leading; instead, he took his "help" from several prevailing cults. We propose to prove this later.

After this lengthy digression, HWA gets back to his life story. He became an "idea man" for his paper; then he conducted public opinion polls in many cities. When one of his reports was printed in the *Journal* he was understandably pleased. His speaking and writing skills developed rapidly. But he kept on shifting from one job to another. The next one was with the South Bend, Indiana, Chamber of Commerce. Here he learned the principle that he could move people to action faster through their emotions than through their reason. He applied this principle and then, "like sheep" he said, his prospects signed.

Leaving South Bend, and personal debts there, he landed in Danville, Illinois, with "not even a dime." But this brash young man soon got a job! And then another job—selling pianos, but he failed to sell even one. Back to Des Moines he went, and to a job with *The Northwestern Banker.* His work was to be with this paper's Chicago office to which he moved in 1915 at age 23. He married Miss Loma Dillon, a third cousin, on July 31, 1917. Their first baby was born the following May. In 1920, his income was about $11,000—not bad for that time and for his age.

Came the depression of 1920-1921 and business disintegrated. Of this time, HWA wrote that his first 28 years of life were "fat years," but the following 28 years were lean and humbling years. From his age of 28 to 35 he and his family were in "virtual poverty" with many unpaid bills. Then he was "converted" and spent seven years in intensive study. Then followed seven more years of poverty and humility; next came growing success with his radio and publications.

In July of 1922 HWA had to give up his Chicago apartment and send his wife and baby girls to her father's farm in Iowa. In

October he followed his wife to Iowa for he could not even pay his own way in Chicago. That winter he helped his brother-in-law, Walter Dillon, win some oratorical contests. Next, he worked at merchandising surveys. Then in the summer of 1924 they moved to his father's new home in Salem, Oregon. In Oregon, more surveys, more failures, and more poverty—even to actual hunger.

Then a neighbor lady induced Mrs. Armstrong to "keep the sabbath." This angered HWA into a frantic study to prove her wrong, so he spent much time in public libraries doing research. They had joined a Methodist church in Maywood, a suburb of Chicago, but this tie was very weak. Within six months he was "converted" and baptized into a very small sabbatarian sect then based in Stanberry, Missouri. The few "Churches of God" in Oregon later formed their own "Oregon Conference" which on March 2, 1932, gave HWA a Ministerial License Certificate "good for one year." This group employed him as an evangelist at $20 per week, but in August of 1933 this salary dwindled to $3 per week. It was over this meager income that two other sabbatarian preachers fought HWA; then HWA gave it up and began to "trust the Lord" for his support. His family suffered greatly meanwhile.

While preaching in a country school house near Eugene, Oregon, he was invited to speak over a 100-watt radio. His voice was good; his message attracted increasing interest; he worked hard, using his considerable talents of persuasive salesmanship; he responded to letters with his mimeographed "Plain Truth" monthly, and he was finally on the way to success!

Mr. Armstrong, after many failures, was to become a super-salesman.

The rapid growth of Armstrongism is largely at the expense of our well established churches. We have a right to defend ourselves against the attacks of Armstrong's many writers and speakers. They call us vicious, evil, and unjust names without reason. When we state the facts about this cult we are not persecuting them. We do expose their many errors and shall continue to do so. We hope their almost-hypnotized members will read us honestly and prayerfully. But most of them are insulated from us in their more-or-less secret meetings which are held only if an authorized agent of Armstrong is present.

They make a show of patriotism but urge their members not to vote! Their reason? Christ did not vote, they say, so we won't! They call their members out from participation in this world and all its affiliations—social, political, economic and religous. Is this being patriotic, or Christian, to let evil men gain control by default, and by our refusing to vote for good men? A British statesman said truly, "All that is needed for evil men to have their way is for good men to do nothing."

Armstrongism can be a real threat to our families, our churches, and to all nations affected by it. HWA calls medicine a form of idolatry (in his "Does God Heal Today?"). He advises against physicians and immunizations, thus endangering the health of loved ones. Suppose we never had any physicians? Christ approved of them in Luke 5:31 and so did Paul in Colossians 4:14. Why shouldn't we? And Armstrongites surely employ dentists on occasion, so where is their consistency?

With all these handicaps against Armstrong, surely he had to be a sort of supersalesman in order to win a following. He is not alone in this. Mohammed did it; Joseph Smith did it for his Mormons; Judge Rutherford did it for his so-called Witnesses; Mrs. Ellen G. White did it for the Adventists, and Father Divine did it for his "angels."

Let us now see how Herbert W. Armstrong has been doing it.

2

A CUNNING SALESMAN'S PSYCHOLOGY

"How much do we owe you for the room?" I asked the lady at the desk. This was at an excellent Bible Institute in Canada where my wife and I had stayed overnight.

"Oh, you don't owe us anything. We only hope you had a good night's rest." This reply, with a sincere Christian smile, captivated us. So—I wrote a check for three times the amount I had expected to pay, and the lady accepted this as a gift to her school. We left with a feeling of good will (and with another deduction from income tax)!

Has Herbert W. Armstrong (HWA) discovered this principle? He tells his readers and hearers over and over again, "This literature is free. You cannot pay for it. Your subscription has been paid for already by generous friends. If you try to pay for yours, we must return your money. And we shall send you any of our publications you ask for—free." Such a sales pitch is sure to snare the unwary. Many send in large gifts, even at the cost of mortgaging their homes.

And when HWA has won a convert, *then* he uses plenty of pressure to extract tithes and offerings from him for life. For his converts are made to believe that they must continue in HWA's teachings—which he seems to equate with his inanimate Holy Spirit—or else suffer the lake of fire.

It is in enticing readers and hearers to *continue* reading and listening that HWA shows his cunning. With five steps he

17

"clinches a sale." (1) Listen to HWA's radio or TV program. (2) Write in for more "information." (3) Ask an Armstrong agent to come, and believe all he says. (4) Attend meetings led by an Armstrong minister. (5) Ask for baptism. Then you are "in"; you are one of the "fortunate" people whom God (HWA) has "called"; you are far superior in knowledge and doctrine to all the preachers in the world!

The Armstrong people are clever writers. By their use of *italics*, CAPITALS, and LARGER CAPITALS, they outshout timid opposition. They drown out doubts by doubling decibels in type. Helpless readers do not answer back to emphatic printing on slick paper, colorful pictures, and artful layout. Those who do not understand such wiles with words are overwhelmed.

Remember, your curiosity could lead you into deeper Armstrong quicksand. To be safe from HWA's voice, write to him: "Cancel this mailing." Enclose your address label, or copy it accurately. His computers will get the message in time. As to radio and TV, it is your will power against his.

> Vice is a monster of such frightful mien,
> As to be hated needs but to be seen.
> Yet, seen too oft, familiar with her face,
> We first endure, then pity, then embrace.
> —Alexander Pope

Armstrong repeats the phrase, "incredible but true," as a stratagem of psychology. It suggests that only he has the ability to discover and describe the knowledge he claims for himself. Then those who believe him share, vicariously, the exaltation of "superior" understanding.

HWA scoffs at the "hundreds of denominations" for their divisions and disagreements, but they are really more united on the Gospel than the scores of cults which continually attack evangelical Christians.

Christian churches have always been easy and inviting targets for critics and fault finders to shoot at. Since no person is perfect, then no church is perfect. But God sees all truly born-again Christians through the precious blood of Christ who forgives us of all our sins.

Surely God loves, intensely, all those whom Christ has saved by His death on the cross. And even though we are very im-

perfect, when Satan attacks us then God defends us. When
King Balak wanted Balaam to curse Israel, the Lord had Balaam
say, "He hath not beheld iniquity in Jacob, neither hath he seen
perverseness in Israel" (Num. 23:21).

But Armstrong fights us. He writes often how bad the world
is, how corruption and crime are growing, and how bad "The
Establishment" is. Then by subtle innuendo, ingenious insinua-
tion, and insidious inference he blames all churches except his
own for the world's ills.

By such cunning literary devices, HWA associates our
churches with the world's "bad guys." Of course he and his
people are the good ones. Then, prospects who are uninformed
or naive are easy prey to HWA's psychological wiles. It is to
warn the unwary that we write.

*   *   *

Professor Fredrick Trautman of Philadelphia's Temple University wrote a discerning article on Armstrong's selling techniques for the magazine *Preaching Today* (March-April, 1971.
Used by permission). It is entitled "From Soap to Souls: The
Armstrongs and 'The World Tomorrow.' " Items:

At age 18, Armstrong studied persuasive language used by a
man who wrote ads for Quaker Oats, Pepsodent, Palmolive,
Ovaltine, and Blue Jay Corn Plasters. Then, according to his
Autobiography, he learned principles of effective advertising and
some rules of persuasion.

First, try hard to persuade.

Second, use prophecy to attract attention and arouse interest. The current interest in astrology and fortune-telling will
help.

Third, cite evidence of God's leading, as often as possible.
Put God on your side and you have it made. HWA told of an
angel steering his car to the home of a dying cripple; then HWA
healed him with prayer!

Fourth, make firm and dogmatic assertions, regardless of the
facts. Make your affirmations simply, clearly, directly, and confidently. Then when you tell your readers that you, of all people,
have the "road map of human destiny," some will believe. Show
your readers that you have the real blueprint of the future, that
after 1900 years of waiting for the right man, God has finally
found him in Herbert W. Armstrong and in his son, Garner Ted!

Fifth, use endless repetition. Begin with the latest news. This lends variety AND the necessary "yes, yes" response from listeners. Mention news accurately; then apply Armstrong's interpretation more or less Biblically, and you can captivate the gullible readily.. This formula seems to satisfy the Armstrongs, for they have been using it since 1934. And it has apparently convinced many listeners. Who else would pay the enormous expenses, estimated at $35,000,000 in 1970, of all the worldwide Armstrong enterprises?

Sixth, there is power in recent and familiar news, when used to demonstrate how God has chosen the Armstrongs as His only vicars on earth. For HWA is not modest or reticent in claiming that he alone has perceived "the truth of man's origin, progress and destiny." Not since 70 A.D. and not until 1934 A.D. has the "Plain Truth" been entrusted to any man. But Armstrong has it—he says!

Seventh, HWA uses the "transfer device," as the Institute for Propaganda Analysis called it. To give news accurately may cast a halo of truth over the whole message. HWA has photographers and reporters all over the world; he has computers in Pasadena to help in processing such news; then they "explain" those news items. So they boast confidently that even our newspapers demonstrate their divine authority! Clever?

Eighth, they use the power of *apparent* rationality. They try to seem plausible. "Let's use our minds . . . Proof . . . Does this seem reasonable? . . . Clear proof . . . Let's think about this . . . scientific proof . . . This stands proved . . . research . . . analysis . . . the logic of this . . . truth . . . You know that is wrong . . . the absolute truth . . . documentation . . . I can prove that . . . objectivity . . . credibility, etc." Persuasive words. They also like to cite authorities, such as encyclopedias, to help narrow their credibility gap. (We shall cite many cases where this gap is wide. SEA.) Armstrong has to trust his people not to "read between the lines."

Ninth, Armstrongites assume a stance of righteousness. They are all against dirt, corruption, and crime. They oppose communism, hippies and intellectuals—especially all clergymen and evangelical scholars. They climb roughshod over the bodies of pastors in order to elevate themselves.

Tenth, Armstrongism offers (1) the sense of belonging to a

group, which together subscribes to the "truth," superior to
other groups and which stands united, warm and friendly against
cold, sinister, inscrutable enemies. (2) A charismatic leader,
H. W. Armstrong, who is shown combining goodness and authority within himself, a man who acts kindly toward the good
and indignantly against the evil, a forceful head of household
and a supporter of law and order—especially God's. (3) Revelation—a set of first principles that, though inexplicable, cannot be
questioned, doubted, or denied, much like Marx's dialectical ma-
terialism, Joseph Smith's visitation by an angel, Hitler's racial
purity and superiority, Euclid's maxims, and the Founding Fathers' "We hold these truths to be self-evident." (4) Explanation
—an ordering of chaos, the answers to all of life's problems, from
how to think to how to act, from how to live to how to die, in
admonitions on nutrition, work, play, hobbies, education, travel,
war, peace, statecraft, love, courtship, marriage, and sex. (5) A
date with destiny, both manifest and global, embracing all man's
past and future.

Professor Trautman adds: It is no laughing matter. Armstrong
used what he had learned selling soap, refined and expanded it,
and now his organization uses it all to appeal to audiences worldwide. The Armstrongs teach a literalistic, millennarian interpretation of the Bible, with themselves as the only true interpreters.
Their techniques and powers of persuasion are many and ingenious . . . They are among the most accomplished God-hucks-
ters of broadcasting.

Still, so long as there are confused Rohans (he set fire to the
Al Aksa Mosque in Jerusalem 8-21-69 while studying Armstrongism), will there not also be bold and adventurous Armstrongs?

Every century has had its self-appointed "prophets" with their
"final" revelations. We shall see that Armstrong is not so new
after all.

3

COMPETING CULTS AND
THIER HIGH COSTS

HERE IS A *partial* list of sects, cults, dissenters, separatists, defectors, seceders or apostates from the original gospel as first given by John the Baptist, Christ, the Apostles, and Paul. The number after each name indicates the century when each movement began. Most of them faded away into nothingness after a very few years.

Christ planted the good seed of the gospel. "But, while men slept, his enemy came and sowed tares among the wheat, and went his way . . . An enemy hath done this" (Matt. 13:24-30). We must not "sleep" any more and thus let enemies continue planting their evil weeds among us.

Elmer T. Clark, *The Small Sects in America* (New York: Abingdon, 1937) lists countless small groups, led by charismatic founders, which lasted only a few years. Most of them insist they are not sects or cults, but they are actually out to rid the world of sects (p. 111)!

Dean M. Kelley, *Why Conservative Churches Are Growing* (New York: Harper & Row, 1972), gives many sharp insights into the peculiar psychology of sects and their dominating leaders. They, like Armstrong, claim to have a monopoly on the truth; they can explain everything; theirs are closed systems needing no help from anyone, for they alone have a pipe line to God!

Dr. A. T. Robertson, *Word Pictures in the New Testament*

(New York: Harper & Row, 1931), commenting on Ephesians 4:14—"That we henceforth be no more children, tossed to and fro, and carried about with every wind of doctrine, by the sleight of men, and cunning craftiness, by which they lie in wait to deceive"—"Some Christians are quite content to remain 'babes' in Christ and never cut their eye-teeth (Heb. 5:11-14), the victims of every charlatan who comes along" (IV, 538).

Adiaphorists	16	Mormons	19
Adoptionists	8	Munsterites	16
Albigenses	13	Mystics	13
Anchorites	4	Naesseri	2
Anglo-Israelites	19	Nestorians	5
Antinomians	16	Occamists	16
Arians	4	Ophites	2
Armstrongites	20	Order of the Star	
Ascetics	4	of the East	20
Bahais	19	Patripassians	2
Beghards	12	Pedobaptists	2
Beguines	12	Pelagians	4
Bollandists	11	Peretai	2
Cainites	2	Psychiana	20
Christadelphians	19	Puseyites	19
Christian Scientists	19	Quakers	17
Cooneyites	19	Raskolniks	17
Deists	17	Restorationists	3
Duothelites	4	Romanists	5
Ebionites	2	Rosicrucians	14
Elkesites	2	Sabellians	2
Euchites	4	Scotists	13
Eusebians	4	Seventh Day Adventists	19
Familists	16	Socinians	16
Father Divine	20	Spiritists	19
Flacians	16	Swedenborgians	18
Gnostics	1	Templars	13
I Am	20	Theophilanthropists	18
Jehovah's Witnesses	19	Theosophists	19
Mandaeans	3	Thomists	13
Manichaeans	2	Ultramontanists	19
Marcionites	2	Unitarians	16
Maronites	4	Unity School	20
Molinists	16	Universalists	18
Monarchians	2	Zen Buddhists	20
Montanists	2	Zoroastrians	4
	Moral Rearmament	20	

The above list is subject to correction. Perhaps some names should be deleted. On the other hand, many cults have come and gone without being noticed by our books on church history.

NOTE: Each devotee of each cult was (is) positive he had (has) the final truth!

Each surviving sect is fighting every other one, but their main target is the mainstream of Christianity—our major denominations and the growing number of independent Bible churches. Against all faithful churches "the gates of hell" shall never prevail (Matt. 16:18). For the Bible was here first. It will outlast all the weeds of all its enemies.

In addition to the 70 groups listed above, we have records of many conflicting philosophies, ideologies and "isms." Dr. Robert G. Lee of Memphis suggested that these "isms should be wasms!" Here are some of them:

Agnosticism	Idealism	Pantheism
Atheism	Instrumentalism	Personalism
Behaviorism	Judaism	Pluralism
Communism	Legalism	Positivism
Darwinism	Liberalism	Realism
Dualism	Materialism	Scholasticism
Empiricism	Mechanism	Scientism
Existentialism	Monism	Transcendentalism
Hedonism	Naturalism	Vitalism
Humanism	Nominalism	

Like cults, smog is a problem. Traffic policemen need gas masks in congested areas. But Christians need not be poisoned by the pollutions of false prophets. To be safe, we must know how to identify various poisons. We shall try to analyze them fairly.

Polluted water is another serious matter. We like to drink pure water, with no contamination in it. Water is often a type of the Word of God (Isa. 12:3; John 3:5; 4:10-15; 7:38; Eph. 5:26; Rev. 7:17; 22:1, 17). We want the "pure river of water of life, clear as crystal" (Rev. 22:1). And who wants Grade C milk?

Cults have contaminated the pure water of life. If readers will look up our many Bible references, they can filter out all contradictions, corruptions and confusing concepts of Armstrong's many additives and/or departures from "the faith which was once delivered unto the saints" (Jude 3).

With unusual frankness Mr. H. W. Armstrong (HWA) confessed a terrible truth in his *Autobiography*, page 331. Referring to a man, or a wife, converted to his beliefs and who tried to persuade the spouse, he said that in all the years since his conversion he knew of dozens and scores of divorces caused by the newly converted mate trying to persuade the other. What a big price to pay! Think of the broken homes, the helpless children, the alienated relatives, and the churches robbed by cultists!

Benjamin Franklin (1706-1790), when he was seven, bought a whistle which he enjoyed briefly, but which annoyed his family. His friends said he paid four times too much for it. They also "put me in mind what good things I might have bought with the rest of the money; and laughed at me so much for my folly, that I cried with vexation . . . As I grew up . . . I met with many, very many, who *gave too much for a whistle*."

Could this be true of Armstrong's followers? They began by paying too much attention to his offer of "free" literature, "free" visits by his trained agents, and his free broadcasts. They cost plenty in the end.

Every salesman of cigarettes, beer, or whisky would gladly give free samples to those who would likely become compulsive users for life.

But the real cost of Armstrongism is not the money they extract from their converts. We give now a partial list of needless sacrifices—some priceless—which HWA demands of his followers.

1. *Do not expect heaven when you die.* That must wait until the resurrection. (We could cite exact paragraph, page and periodical for each point, but we dislike advertising any cult's materials.) Here HWA follows back-slidden Solomon who said a man dies like a beast, no difference (Eccl. 3:19, 20). How bleak is such an outlook. HWA also teaches that the day of one's death is better than the day of birth (Eccl. 7:1)! But I prefer to believe Christ: a dying Christian does go to heaven (Matt. 22:31, 32; Luke 23:43; Acts 7:55-60; 2 Cor. 5:1-10; Phil. 1:23). HWA says one is *totally* dead until the resurrection, but the New Testament (NT) says no. More on this in chapter 31.

2. *Reject the Holy Spirit as a Person,* HWA insists. He speaks "against the Holy Spirit" (Matt. 12:32), by downgrading Him from Personality to a force, or influence, or an inanimate "it."

To deny the Personality of the Holy Spirit is to (1) negate our means of salvation (John 3:5); (2) downgrade the inspiration of the Bible (2 Peter 1:21); (3) deny the administrative work of the Spirit during our church age (Acts 13:2, 24; 21:11);

(4) deny the deity of the Holy Spirit (Acts 5:3, 4); and (5) deny the ability of the Holy Spirit to think, prophesy, or command. More on this in chapter 25.

3. *Fall from grace to Old Testament law.* The Galatians trusted partly in Christ and partly in circumcision. Armstrong trusts largely in sabbath-keeping and in observing the Old Testament feasts. These were shadows or patterns of the realities to follow in the New Testament era. It is like a woman preferring to wear a pattern instead of the finished dress made according to the pattern. Either way, such legalism is "falling from grace" (Gal. 5:4). More on this.

4. *Accept shackles of legalism for life.* Paul tried his best to rescue the Galatians from their legalism. "O foolish Galatians, who hath bewitched you, that ye should not obey the truth?" HWA says, "Back to OT laws!" But Paul said, "How turn ye again to the weak and beggarly elements unto which ye desire again to be in bondage" (Gal. 4:9)?

5. *All Sundays are taboos,* 52 of them each year. We must not worship the sun, says HWA! As though any Christian does, though the sun IS a type of God (Psalm 84:11), and of Christ (Mal. 4:2). And the sun is better that Saturn (Saturday, HWA's big day), or Monday for the moon, or Tuesday for the pagan Tiw, or Wednesday for Woden, or Thursday for Thor, or Friday for Frigga. More on this in chapter 8.

6. *Give up all faith in pastors and scholars,* says HWA. What if they are devout, Spirit-filled, honest, intelligent, unselfish, fruitful, honorable and God-called? If they worship on Sunday they are out.

7. *HWA says that most churches are Satan-worshipers,* and must be shunned. He reverses the NT guideposts, even as Hallowe'en pranksters have done. As a boy with a friend on a long bicycle trip to a distant church, on November first, we saw a reversed road sign. How did we know? We knew where we came from, and we knew the general direction of our goal. Now if two boys could not be deceived by such a simple trick, why should adult Christians be deceived by HWA who changes so many signs? "Cursed be he who removeth his neighbor's landmark" (Deut. 27:17; Job 24:2; Prov. 22:28).

8. *Stop all religious reading except Armstrongism.* If Armstrongites read Christian books and magazines—or Bibles—they

must use HWA's filter to keep out "the liberty with which Christ has made us free" (Gal. 5:1). The Book of Galatians was written especially to free all Christians from legalism which is very similar to the OT Jewish laws of Armstrong.

9. *Turn off all religious radio and TV*, except HWA. He means ALL radio and TV preachers who fail to follow his OT sabbath rules. And he also rejects Seventh Day Adventists, for they do not keep the Jewish feasts, and they refuse to recognize HWA as a new prophet.

10. *Repudiate most Christian hymns.* Armstrongites must avoid the lovely Spirit-filled hymns of the Wesleys, Toplady, Watts, Crosby, Towner, Stebbins, Sankey, Bliss, Bennard, Peterson and hosts of others. HWA rules them out of the Christian fold; yet in his spiritual poverty he uses some of our common hymns. A friend asked how they could do this.

Mr. W. A. Berg replied for HWA. "If a proper hymn is used to worship a so-called "god" on Sunday it would be in vain, since Sunday is not the day God ordained for worship. But if the same proper hymn were used on the true sabbath, God would accept such worship if it were being offered in the sincerity of people's hearts."

My friend replied, "Why is it wrong to worship God on Sunday, or any other day of the week? Do you limit your people to singing hymns or listening to music on only one day a week? Jesus sang with His disciples at the Last Supper, sometime in the middle of the week. If it is a sin to worship God on Sunday, what then is to be our attitude to God on that day?

"In our church we sing hymns like 'All Hail the Power of Jesus' Name,' 'Beautiful Savior,' 'Crown Him Lord of All,' etc. We cannot possibly sing these to, or about, Satan. The person who wrote these hymns wrote them about Christ, not Satan; and the people that sing them, sing them in praise to Christ whom we know as our Savior." (Mr. Berg failed to reply.)

11. *Discard all previous Christian heroes.* This means such saintly men and women as John and Charles Wesley, Whitefield, Spurgeon, Finney, Moody, Fanny Crosby, Mary Slessor, Lottie Moon, and all current Christian leaders who do not follow Armstrong. Yet HWA cited George Mueller (1805-1898) as his best example of a man of prayer. He did colossal work in England with his orphanages, feeding many thousands of children,

depending only on God through prayer. He was truly a good and saintly man.

A friend wrote to the Armstrongs, asking if Mueller was a Christian.

"No, we do not feel that he was," came the reply 4-26-71. "To our knowledge, Mr. Mueller did not have God's Spirit in him and therefore was not a true Christian (Rom. 8:9) . . . he was obeying Satan's counterfeits, which, again, he undoubtedly thought were of God."

So one of God's very greatest saints, one extremely useful, one full of the Holy Spirit if ever anyone was, one respected and loved by millions of true Christians—even he is ruled out by HWA's rigid legalism.

12. *Cut off the Christian part* of your Christian friends and relatives, even those trusted and tried and true for many years. The Law of Armstrong says you may keep them as friends, but not as Christians, for all worshippers on Sundays are devil-bound (says HWA).

13. *Cancel all evangelistic efforts.* HWA says that Christ did not try to "convert men's souls!" (But He did, as we show later.) And HWA spends many millions of dollars on proselyting, much of that money from people who previously had given to our true gospel churches and missions.

14. *Enroll as one more cultist.* Each cultist is *sure* he has the final truth! Armstrongism is a cult; it depends on one man and his successors; it opposes 99.9% of Christendom.

15. *Become a fetus for Armstrong.* He insists that no one is really born again until the resurrection; until then he is merely "begotten," and only a fetus. More on this strange fantasy later.

16. *Deposit all your religion with Armstrong*—or else! Only those who remain faithful to Armstrongism until death can hope for a happy resurrection. HWA dictates beliefs, policies, tithes, feasts—all from Pasadena. When HWA passes away, his son is likely to take over the rulership.

17. *No more birthday celebrations!* No more cards or cakes or company, says HWA. Why? (See our chapter 36 on this.) It may seem trivial, but it shows clearly how these cultists' lives are minutely controlled. Who knows how many more taboos, rules, restrictions and "no-no's" will come?

18. *Cancel Christmas as all pagan.* Do not buy, send, or read

Christmas cards, even if they have Bible verses or pictures on them. Reason: no Christmas is authorized in the Bible, and the date has a hazy connection with an ancient pagan feast. So—no Christmas presents, programs, songs, trees, decorations, or rejoicing. No Christmas joys for children! This is the decree from Armstrong, and it must be obeyed by his faithful.

In contrast, read the Bible on the extravagant joy at Christ's birth. The wise men "rejoiced with exceeding great joy" (Matt. 2:10), and they gave Him precious gifts. Elizabeth rejoiced, and John the Baptist "leaped . . . for joy" (Luke 1:41-45). Mary rejoiced (Luke 1:46-55); the angels rejoiced (Luke 2:9-14); shepherds rejoiced (Luke 2:15-20); so did Simeon and Anna (Luke 2:25-38). Why, then, should not *all Christians* celebrate each Christmas, thus adding to the worldwide testimony of our Lord Jesus?

Why should the exact date matter? It is the great event, not the date, that has such tremendous meaning for us who love Christ. England's Queen Elizabeth was born April 21, but her birthday is celebrated in June. And it is better to celebrate Christ's birthday in December than not at all.

Mr. Armstrong, instead of enjoying Christmas, seems to enjoy exalting whatever paganism he can find in the Dark Ages or before. He thinks this paganism has deceived Christendom. The fact is, evangelical Christians have defeated 99% of any real or imagined pagan backgrounds of Christmas.

HWA blunders badly in his booklet on "The Plain Truth about Christmas." He tries to trace this glad day back to Nimrod of Genesis 10; he *knows* Nimrod's birthday was December 25; that his name means "he rebelled" but it really means "valiant" or "strong." Worse, he has Nimrod married to Semiramis who lived about 1400 years *later!* He also says the son of Isis was born December 25; yet he is positive that Christ was not born on that date. His history is as dubious as his theology.

Now we do not need holly, or mistletoe, or Santa Claus—if he eclipses Christ even a little. But HWA throws the baby out with the bath water!

19. *Avoid Easter like the plague*, says HWA. He is especially severe in attacking this day so meaningful for hundreds of millions of Christians. On this great day Christ receives worldwide honor and witness, but HWA wants to kill all that. He tries to

elevate "Ishtar" as the controlling power over all Sunday-keeping Christians. On the contrary, Christ has conquered this false god, and many others. (More on this in chapter 9.)

20. *New Year's Day must go,* says HWA. No cards, gifts, or visits. The reason: it is connected with the ancient Julian (Roman) calendar, and HWA wants the older Jewish calendar. So he joins with Christ-rejecting Jews in his condemnation of over 50 of our annual holy days and holidays.

The above 20 points are only part of the price which all converts to Armstrongism must pay. Many of these items will be clarified in later chapters. The acid test of Scripture will be applied to each one. In the meantime, one wonders how HWA can "sell" such a bill of non-goods, or negatives, to anyone who reads his Bible carefully.

But Herbert Armstrong has been learning and practicing clever psychological selling-strategies for 60 years. By now he has also taught his writers those same subtle skills. They take an isolated verse of Scripture and then build an inverted pyramid of false doctrine upon it. But—we shall compare Scripture with Scripture and thus analyze their errors. Satan quoted Scripture to Christ (Matt. 4:1-11), but Christ countered successfully with stronger and more relevant verses. We shall try to do just what Christ did: show that the Bible does not support false doctrines.

4

DOES THE BIBLE
SUPPORT ARMSTRONGISM?

GOD's *moral* LAWS are ageless; that is, it has always been wrong
to lie, murder, steal or swear. Cain's murder of Abel was as evil
before the Ten Commandments were given through Moses as
afterwards.

But in a desperate effort to prove that the Mosaic laws of the
Old Testament are still in full force upon all Christians now,
Armstrong's writers resort to questionable (if not dishonest)
practices.

Their chief aim seems to be to emphasize the fourth commandment concerning the Jewish Sabbath. Failure to observe
this seventh day, they say, is disobedience to God, and thus it
means the loss of salvation.

But since we have a NEW Testament, it *must* mean that it is
different from, and better for us than, the Old Testament. The
NT repeats nine commandments in different ways, and improves
on the fourth one by giving us the First Day as our new holy
day. More on this in chapters 8 and 9.

Dr. D. M. Panton wrote in *Heresies Exposed* (compiled by
A. C. Irvine, 7th edition, 1930, Moody Press):

> I, as a Christian, obey all law that is moral in the Decalogue,
> not because it is in the law, *but because it is in the Gospel.*
> Worship of God only is enjoined 50 times in the NT; idolatry is
> forbidden 12 times; profanity four times; honor of father and
> mother is commanded 6 times; adultery is forbidden 12; theft 6;

31

false witness 4; and covetousness 9 times. . . . So therefore Paul, in all his 14 epistles never once names the Sabbath—except in a single passage where, classing it with the entire law, he declares it has been totally abolished. So the early church held.

Dr. Roy L. Aldrich, writing on "Has the Mosaic Law Been Abolished?" in the October, 1959 *Bibliotheca Sacra,* says that the entire Mosaic Law is a unit, with no division between moral and ceremonial, and that it is all done away. He cites 2 Corinthians 3:6-13 as one text among many. For the Ten Commandments were a part of the civil, or legal, system of Israel as a theocracy. That theocracy ended long ago. But God's eternal moral laws are always in effect, even though Mosaism was only for one epoch.

Rev. D. M. Canright, in his *Seventh Day Adventism Renounced,* p. 320 (Revell) was very thorough in saying that the OT law was for Israel only.

> *The law was given only to the Jews.* This is so manifest in every item of the law, that it needs no agrument to prove it. Moses said (Deut. 4:8) that *no nation* has a law so good "as all this law which I set *before you* this day." Then he names the ten commandments as a part of it, verses 10–13. "This is the law which Moses set before the children of Israel" (v. 44). Before whom? Israel, not the Gentiles. So again, 5:1, "Hear, O Israel, the statutes and judgments which I speak in your ears." Then follows the decalogue. So it is a hundred times over all through the law. It is addressed to the Jews and to them only. The very wording of the law shows it was designed for them only. The decalogue is introduced thus: "I am the Lord thy God, *which brought thee out of the land of Egypt,* out of the house of bondage" (Exo. 20:2). To whom is that applicable? Only to the Jewish nation. Neither angels, Adam, nor Gentile Christians were ever in Egyptian bondage. Then this law is not addressed to them. To whom was the law given? Let Paul answer, in Romans 9:4. It was given to Israel. "Remember ye the law of Moses my servant, which I commanded him in Horeb for all Israel with the statutes and judgments" (Mal. 4:4). The law was *"for all Israel,"* and for them only.
>
> *The Gentiles did not have the law.* This has been proved already; but Paul directly says so (Rom. 2:14). "For when the Gentiles, *which have not the law,* do by nature the things contained in the law, *these having not the law,* are a law unto themselves." This is too plain to need arguing. The Gentiles did not have the law. Paul says so directly and that ought to settle

it, and does. To understand and obey the great moral principles of that law is one thing; to be under the letter, the exact wording of the law as given in detail on Sinai is quite another. . ."

The Bible further contradicts Armstrongism in 2 Corinthians 3:16-17. In an article by Armstrongite R. C. Meredith entitled, "Is Obedience to God Required for Salvation?" an effort is made to connect 2 Corinthians 3:16-17 with other laws on the "whole stones" of Deuteronomy 27:1-8. Here Armstrongism uses the well known strategy of magicians: they divert attention from one thing to another, and thus deceive onlookers. Naturalists tell us a cat twitches the end of its tail to detract attention of its prey. A tiger does the same, with its tail-tip eight feet from its fangs, while stalking an animal or a man. Now look at 2 Corinthians 3:6-17.

Notice, Moses' face shone in connection with the Ten Commandments (Exo. 34:28-35; Deut. 5:22; 9:9-11). His face did *not* shine in connection with the laws of Deuteronomy 27:1-6, which Armstrongism *wrongly* says is discussed in 2 Corinthians 3:6-17.

The Ten Commandments were "written and engraved in stones" (2 Cor. 3:7), (these were *hewn* stones, Exodus 34:1, 4) *but* the commandments of Deuteronomy 27:1-6 were written— *not* engraved—in plaster over *whole* stones.

"The letter killeth" (2 Cor. 3:6) refers to the OT laws (Rom. 2:29; 7:6; 2:27). This is replaced in the NT by the Spirit who gives life.

The Ten Commandments are called the "ministration of death" (2 Cor. 3:7) and "of condemnation" (v. 9). They are replaced now by "the ministration of the Spirit" (v. 8) and "of righteousness" (v. 9). Again, the new covenant is better than the old. (R. C. Meredith tries to say that "only the ministration of death" was abolished, not the Ten Commandments. But the "ministration of death" WAS engraved on stones; it WAS the Ten Commandments. And since their violation meant death, their identity is doubly certain.)

This "ministration of death" refers to the Mosaic *theocracy* which was then empowered to impose capital punishment for violation of the decalogue. Since no church now—Armstrong's or Seventh Dayists'—can execute a sabbath breaker, then their sabbath "law" is of no effect.

The old laws had their time of glory for they came from God to Moses, but that glory "was to be done away." In contrast, the NT does now "exceed in glory"; "much more that which remaineth is glorious" (v. 11).

The changeable moon has its glory on clear nights, but when the sun rises the moon's temporary glory is "done away." Now why should any NT Christian go back to the pale moon of OT legalism, when the "Sun of righteousness has arisen with healing in his wings" (Mal. 4:2)? So—Christ's new commandments are thus better than the old ones of Moses.

We see then that the Ten Commandment law is "that which is done away" (2 Cor. 3:11), and "that which is abolished" (v. 13). And the NT has higher and better laws, as well as a better rest day.

The unconverted Jews of Paul's day were blinded to the NEW Testament of Christ (vs. 13-16). "The veil is upon their hearts" (v. 15). Even so, Armstrongites and Christ-rejecting Jews are now blinded by their veils of legalism from accepting the NEW Covenant (vs. 14-18; Heb. 8:6, 7, 13).

Armstrongism is built on such errors. It is built on bubbles.

And Armstrong's writers depend on the tendency of most readers NOT to check on the accuracy of their unsupported assertions. A careful reading of the few texts involved shows that the Bible does not support Armstrongism. And we surely know that the NT laws are better than OT laws.

Our NT Sundays do not cancel respect for the creation which the OT sabbaths honored (Exo. 20:11). But sabbath-keeping DOES cancel respect for the NT Resurrection Day of our Lord and Savior Jesus Christ.

✿ ✿ ✿

Armstrong relies heavily on his faulty interpretation of 1 John 3:4, "Whosoever committeth sin transgresseth also the law; for sin is the transgression of the law."

The literal (Greek) reading is, "Everyone that practices sin also practices lawlessness (*anomia*), for sin is lawlessness."

The NT use of the word "law" never means the ten commandments alone, much less the fourth one. Canright: "The word 'law' occurs in the Bible over 400 times, yet in not one single instance is the decalogue as a whole or alone called 'the law.' "

"No Sabbatarian, therefore, 'keeps the law,' 'the law of God,' or 'the law of the Lord,' for if he did he would offer sacrifices, be circumcised, and live exactly as the Jews did" (*Ibid.*, p. 316).

By the time John wrote his first epistle of love, at about 85 A.D., his Christian readers were quite well established in NEW Testament ways of living. The old dispensation had passed away (Heb. 8:6-13).

In First John, the word "commandments" refers to *Christ's* commands, *not* to those given through Moses (John 1:17). Notice how very clear this is in 1 John 2:3, 4, 7, 8; 3:22-24; 4:21; 5:2, 3; also in John 13:34 and 15:12.

In spite of all this, HWA repeats often that 1 John 3:4 means that any one not keeping the sabbath will go into the lake of fire.

Church historians are practically unanimous in saying that the early Christians honored the first day of the week, beginning with the glorious Day of Resurrection. Also, some apparently respected the old Jewish sabbaths for a few years as well. The transition from old to new occurred gradually, as was to be expected. More on this in chapter 8.

We can be very sure, then, that John who also wrote John 1:17 would not want his readers, including us now, to go back into Jewish bondage. The NT "commandments are not grievous" (1 John 5:3), but the OT laws were a "Yoke . . . which neither our fathers nor we were able to bear" (Acts 15:10).

⁕ ⁕ ⁕

Mr. R. C. Meredith (RCM) accuses gospel preachers of saying it is no longer needful to obey God, since we leave the old Jewish laws of a former dispensation. This is quite unfair of him. For NT preachers have a higher law than RCM's Jewish commandments. And in downgrading our preachers—those faithful men who try hard to maintain respect for law and order—Armstrongism is actually on the side of the law breakers.

Mr. RCM is badly confused in saying that the Israelites were unable to understand spiritual things, yet on the same page he said the Ten Commandments were spiritual laws! If the Israelites could not understand spiritual matters, of what use to them were the Psalms?

And he repeats the notion that the Israelites were not converted, and had no chance of eternal life in that age. He tries, vainly, to show that God does not plan to save many people until the resurrection!

Countering Armstrongism, the Book of Galatians shows to all

legalists, then and now, the utter folly of going back to "the weak and beggarly elements" of the OT law, after having once enjoyed the glorious liberty of the grace of Jesus Christ.

The new Scofield Reference Bible, which we use, corrects the faulty King James Version of 1 Corinthians 9:20. It should be, "And unto the Jews I became as a Jew, that I might gain the Jews; to them that are under the law, as under the law, *not being myself under the law,* that I might gain them that are under the law." This bursts another Armstrong support.

If only the Armstrongites understood this verse they would save themselves, and their readers, much needless confusion.

But Armstrongism says the Ten Commandments were not written on stones, nor were they superseded by NT laws. The *Bible* says, "And the Lord said to Moses, Hew thee two tables of stone like unto the first; and I will write upon these tables the words that were in the first tables" (Exo. 34:1). "And he (God) wrote upon the tables the words of the covenant, the ten commandments" (Exo. 34:28). Then in Exodus 34:29, 30, 33-35 we read that the "skin of Moses' face shone" so that "he put a veil on his face." So—2 Corinthians 3:6-17 *does* refer to the Ten Commandents, regardless of the irresponsible writings of Armstrongism.

*   *   *

In the same vein as the Meredith article, there is one by R. C. Cole, "The New Covenant—Does It Abolish God's Law?"

Mr. Cole maligns NT preachers when he accuses us of saying that we all want the liberty of doing whatever we please. Not so.

Regarding Hebrews 8:7, 8 he fails to notice that it says the first covenant was not faultless. For him to do so would have undermined his argument, and it would have cancelled the need for a second covenant.

He admits that the old covenant was a marriage agreement between God and OT Israel, but he fails to mention what Paul wrote on this, that the old covenant died, and therefore NT Israel—and we—are free "to marry another," even Christ. This is made very clear in Romans 7:1-7.

And contrary to Cole, God DID command Israel concerning burnt offerings and sacrifices immediately after giving them the decalogue. Exodus 20:18-24 makes this clear enough.

Mr. Cole, as most legalists, tries hard to separate the ceremonial and ritualistic parts of the Mosaic Code from the Ten Commandments, but James 2:10 will not allow it. "For whosoever shall keep the whole law, and yet offend in one point, he is guilty of all."

Armstrongism insists that God did not give any spiritual promises to Israel, only material ones, and that they did not have the Holy Spirit. But Psalm 51:11—"take not thy Holy Spirit from me"—indicates otherwise, and the Psalms are filled with wonderful spiritual promises.

Mr. Cole seems worse confused in saying that the New Covenant will not include Gentiles. But the NT contradicts him. John the Baptist said of Christ in John 1:29, "Behold the Lamb of God who taketh away the sin *of the world.*" Any concordance reveals the fact that the NT gospel is for the whole world. And Acts 15 says the Gentiles (contrary to Cole) are to be saved apart from Israel. The Conference at Jerusalem declared all Christians to be free from OT laws and ceremonies.

And Mr. Cole says no one is saved, or belongs to Christ, until he is baptized. But the repentant thief was saved without baptism, and Saul of Tarsus was saved three days before his baptism.

The new covenant, says Mr. Cole, is not yet complete, but John 17:4, 19:30 and Hebrews 1:3 all say that it is.

Another grievous error: Mr. Cole says that we are not born again until the resurrection. But see 2 Peter 1:23; 1 John 2:29; 3:9; 4:7; 5:1, 4, 18. When a person receives Christ (John 1:12) he THEN receives a new, heavenly nature—one that cannot sin. 1 John 3:9 calls this new nature "his seed," and it is only this divine part of a Christian which cannot sin. The two natures are described in Galatians 5:16-23. The new nature is permanently implanted within us the moment we receive Christ as Savior and Lord (Rom. 10:9; Eph. 2:8; 2 Peter 1:4; John 3:5, etc.). So, each Christian has the new divine nature NOW.

Mr. Cole thinks the church is Israel; this is also confusing and wrong. He is anxious to put us back into the bondage of Jewish laws. But we can not, and need not, become "Israelites" in order to be saved.

But if the Mosaic laws are not for us, what was their purpose? Items—

1. To reveal the holiness of God (1 Peter 1:15).

2. To expose the sinfulness of man (Gal. ,3:19).

3. To present a standard of holiness for Israel (Psalm 24:3-5).

4. To train and discipline immature children of Israel (Gal. 3:24).

5. To unify Israel as a nation, a theocracy (Exo. 19:5-8; Deut. 5:27, 28).

6. To separate, set apart, and distinguish Israel from all other nations (Exo. 31:13-17).

7. To provide for sacrifices, forgiveness, and fellowship (Lev. 1-7).

8. To provide a way to worship God (Lev. 23).

9. To reveal, or test, each Israelite's relationship to God (Deut. 28).

10. To reveal Jesus Christ (Luke 24:44, 45). Now since Christ *has come,* we Gentiles have all these purposes *fulfilled in Him.* This makes Romans 7:12 and 1 Timothy 1:8 clear; the Mosaic law had its uses for Israel, but it has different (exemplary) uses for Christians now.

Since the word "law" has so many meanings in Scripture, Armstrong's writers can use the word in loose, ambiguous, and misleading ways. The word has about 12 different connotations in the Bible. Items—

1. The Pentateuch (Luke 24:44).

2. The Old Testament (John 12:34; 15:25).

3. The Mosaic law (Matt. 22:37-40).

4. Civil Government laws (Prov. 28:4).

5. Psychological law (Rom. 7:23, 25).

6. Some particular regulation (John 19:7).

7. The ceremonial aspect (Heb. 7:28; 8:4; 9:22).

8. Law as principle (Rom. 3:27; 8:2).

9. Law in general (Rom. 7:1, 2).

10. Law as penalty (Rom. 4:15; Gal. 3:10).

11. Law as contrasted to grace (Matt. 23:23; Gal. 3:11).

12. The law of Christ (Gal. 6:2; James 1:25; 2:12).

Scripture, then, does not support Armstrongism when it condemns us for worshiping on Sundays. Since Armstrong's emphasis on sabbath-keeping is mentioned by him so often, and since it is one key to his many other quirks of doctrine, we must repeat our defenses.

If one "declaration of independence" from Jewish legalism is not enough for Armstrong, we can supply scores of them!

Next, then, let us read some clear NT statements which declare that we are now free from the bonds of Jewish-Armstrong legalism.

But first, notice how Armstrong's writers build inverted pyramids on obscure and difficult verses; then they twist clear verses to conform to their peculiar views. "What is at first a bare possibility, is turned into a surmise; a surmise soon becomes a likelihood; the likelihood becomes an extreme probability and ends by becoming a dogmatic certainty!" This is how Armstrong tries to deceive. (from *Heresies Exposed,* 7th Ed., p. 25.)

5

GOD'S SUPREME COURT
REJECTS ARMSTRONGISM

THE DIVINE CONSTITUTION for Christian people and churches is
the New Testament. This is the new Covenant, or Contract, or
Will. As an original will is changed by a new one, or by a
codicil, so the Old Testament has been amended for us by the
New Testament.

Now Christ "is the mediator of the new testament" and "a
testament is of force after men are dead; otherwise it is of no
strength at all while the testator liveth" (Heb. 9:15-17). When
Christ died, the old testament was finally displaced by the new
one. The old, which contained the Mosaic laws of sabbaths and
Levitical feasts, was now "done away." But God's eternal laws
against murder, lying, and stealing are always the same.

Even before the Cross, John the Baptist and Christ and His
apostles were preaching the new principles of our NT Constitution. But for Jews who took fanatical pride in their legal traditions, this change was hard to accept. The unconverted Jews
fought this change so hard that they managed to have Christ
crucified.

Some converted Jews—not all—fought this change also. Acts
15:24 tells of Jewish legalists—like Armstrong—who "troubled
you with words, subverting your souls, saying, Ye must be circumcised, and keep the law . . ." Armstrong conveniently skips
circumcision but he "subverts" people by his insistence on other
Jewish laws. (To subvert means to overthrow, to ruin utterly,
to corrupt, to undermine the allegiance or faith of people.)

These legalists raised such a dissension that the church at Antioch sent a delegation, including Paul and Barnabas, to the apostles and elders of the Jerusalem church. They wanted this matter settled once for all. The apostles and elders were the Supreme Court for these Christians. They had been with Christ (Acts 1:21, 22); they knew His mind (1 Cor. 2:16; Phil. 2:5), and they were loyal to Him (Acts 15:11, 26).

The Supreme Court of the United States works hard to interpret the Constitution of our country. They decide questions on which two or more opposing groups differ. And their decision is final. But before we look into Acts 15, let us review some fundamental principles of the Christians' Constitution (the NT) on which the Supreme Court gave its verdict.

Matthew 4:23 "And Jesus went . . . preaching the *gospel.*" The gospel is GOOD NEWS; it is *better* than OT laws (Heb. 7:19, 22; 8:6; 9:23); it frees us from OT bondage in each of the 101 times "gospel" is found in the NT.

Matthew 9:16, 17 "Do not patch new cloth (NT) with old cloth (OT)."

Matthew 12:8 "For the Son of man is Lord even of the sabbath day." He *had the right* to give us a new day for worship, a better day, meaning more.

Matthew 23:36-40 "Love to God and man covers all OT laws," Jesus said.

Matthew 26:28 "For this is my blood of the NEW TESTAMENT . . ." So Jesus signed our NT Constitution with His own blood. Let us accept it, fully.

Mark 1:1 "The beginning of the gospel of Jesus Christ, the Son of God" Then the Old Testament laws had to end at the beginning of the gospel.

Luke 16:16 "The law and the prophets were until John (the Baptist)" and he was the first preacher in the New Testament.

Luke 24:44 Jesus said, ". . . all things must be fulfilled, which were written in the law of Moses . . ." Since Christ fulfilled the OT laws, we do not need to; we couldn't, anyway. He did it all FOR us. We have broken the Mosaic laws, but Christ paid the penalty for us. He died for us. We, too, die symbolically in our baptism (Rom. 6:4; Col. 2:12), and such death *frees us* from OT laws (Rom. 7:1-7). In Christ, we now have higher and better laws which can, and should, make us better people.

John 1:17 "For the law was given by Moses, but grace and truth came by Jesus Christ." So the OT law *ended* when Christ came. Here it is law OR grace, Moses OR Christ; it is not "both-and" as Armstrong says. Paul emphasizes this "either-or" cleavage in Galatians 5:1-4.

John 10:28 "I *give* unto them eternal life." We do not earn salvation by observing OT sabbaths and feasts, nor do we retain it that way.

John 13:34 "A new commandment I give unto you, that ye love one another . . ." Love is the fulfilling of the law (Rom. 13:8, 10). This NT law is *new;* it is new both in time and in quality.

John 17:4 "I have finished the work." John 19:30 "It is finished." Hebrews 1:3 "by himself He purged our sins." Christ finished ALL the demands of the OT laws upon us, and on all mankind.

Acts 6:14 Stephen was killed because the Jews said he would "change the customs which Moses delivered us." Christ was killed for the same reason, for He violated their sabbath rules. Paul was hounded constantly because he failed to keep the Jewish rules. If these three had been Armstrongites, they might not have been persecuted!

Acts 10:12-15 God gave Peter a special revelation to show that OT laws were changed or abolished, including dietary laws.

Acts 13:39 "And by him (Christ) all that believe are justified from ALL things, from which ye could not be justified by the law of Moses." Isn't this far better than Armstrong's legalism?

Acts 15:1 Certain men *troubled* Gentile Christians with Mosaic laws, much like Armstrong's agents do now. These men debated Paul and Barnabas.

Acts 15:2 The Supreme Court of the early Christian churches was the Twelve Apostles and the elders in Jerusalem. They "tried" the case of "Legalism vs the NT Gospel of Liberty," Acts 15:3-18. Legalism lost, Acts 15:19-29. Even so, the "Case of Armstrong vs the New Testament" is lost.

Acts 15:5 "But there rose up certain of the sect of the Pharisees, who believed, saying it was needful . . . to keep the law of Moses." So now Armstrong's agents go around the world with their pharisaical confusion.

Acts 15:10 "Now, therefore, why tempt ye God, to *put a yoke* upon the neck of the disciples, *which neither our fathers nor we were able to bear?"* This "yoke" is the Mosaic law, contrary to which "we believe that through the grace of the Lord Jesus Christ we shall be saved, even as they" (v. 11). So we are now saved *apart from* the OT law. Compare 1 John 5:3.

Acts 15:24 "certain . . . have troubled you with words, subverting your souls, saying, Ye must . . . keep the law, *to whom we gave no such commandment."* Anyone can read this loud and clear.

Acts 15:28, 29 "For it seemed good to the Holy Spirit, and to us, to lay upon you no greater burden than these necessary things (of v. 29)." Here was a happy deliverance from the burdens and bonds of OT laws.

Acts 18:13; 21:21-28 Paul was persecuted regarding OT laws.

Now Paul explains our NT freedom from OT legalism:

Romans 2:14 ". . . the Gentiles, who have not the law . . ."

Romans 3:21 "by the deeds of the law shall no flesh be justified."

Romans 3:21 "the righteousness of God apart from the law is manifested"

Romans 3:28 "a man is justified by faith apart from the deeds of the law"

Romans 3:31 "we establish the law" How? By being in Christ who established the law when He died to pay all penalties of all OT laws. We could not pay all those penalties ourselves. Christ did; so IN Christ all are free from OT law. Apart from Him we are still bound in sins.

Romans 4:2-7 Even Abraham was not justified by works!

Romans 4:13, 14 "the promise . . . was not to Abraham, or to his seed, through the law, but through the righteousness of faith. For if they who are of the law be heirs, faith is made void." It is law OR faith.

Romans 5:1 "being justified by faith, we have peace with God."

Romans 6:14, 15 "for ye are not under law, but under grace."

Romans 7:3 "she (widow to law) is free from that law."

Romans 7:4 "ye also are become dead to the law by the body of Christ."

Romans 7:6 "But now we are delivered from the law, that being dead in which (law) we were held, that we should serve in newness of spirit and not in oldness of the letter (or OT laws)."

Romans 7:12 "Wherefore, the law is holy, and the commandment holy, and just and good." Of course; the law was good for its dispensation. It served its purpose until Christ came with His better laws. When penalties for breaking OT laws are no longer in force, such as stoning anyone for gathering sticks on a sabbath day, then such "law" is no more than advice!

Romans 8:2 "For the law of the Spirit of life in Christ Jesus hath made me free from the law (OT) of sin and death. We who are IN Christ (v. 3, 4) have met all demands of the OT law, vicariously.

Romans 9:31, 32 "Righteousness is impossible by works of the law."

Romans 10:4 "For Christ is the end of the law for righteousness to everyone that believeth." How could it be clearer than that?

Romans 13:8, 10 "he that loveth another hath fulfilled the law."

Romans 14:5, 6 frees us from OT sabbaths and feast days. Romans 14:2, 3; 1 Corinthians 10:25-27 and 1 Timothy 4:1-5 cancel OT taboos on pork!

1 Corinthians 14:34, 35 Armstrong's wife led him into sabbatarianism and legalism; Eve led Adam astray; Miriam led her brother Aaron into rebellion, and Delilah wore Samson into submission within a week.

The Book of Galatians is our Magna Charta against Armstrongism.

Galatians 1:6, 7 "I marvel that ye are so soon removed from him that called you into the grace of Christ unto another gospel, which is not another; but there are some (OT legalists) that trouble you, and would pervert (turn away from) the gospel of Christ." Like Armstrongites.

Galatians 2:16 "Knowing that a man is not justified by the works of the law, but by the faith in Jesus Christ . . . and not by the works of the law; for by the works of the law shall no flesh be justified."

Galatians 2:19 "For I, through the law, am dead to the law . . ."

Galatians 2:21 "If righteousness come by the law, then Christ is dead in vain." Legalists say: Christ died in vain. Awful!

Galatians 3:3 "Are ye so foolish? Having begun in the Spirit, are ye now made perfect by the flesh (or by OT laws)?"

Galatians 3:5 "by the works of the law, OR by the hearing of faith?"

Galatians 3:10 "For as many as are of the works of the law are under the curse; for it is written, Cursed is everyone that continueth not in all things which are written in the book of the law, to do them."

Galatians 3:11 "no man is justified by the law in the sight of God"

Galatians 3:13 "Christ hath redeemed us from the curse of the law"

Galatians 3:23 "But before faith came, we were kept under the law"

Galatians 3:24, 25 "The law was our schoolmaster to bring us unto Christ, that we might be justified by faith. But after that faith is come, we are no longer under a schoolmaster."

Galatians 4:9 "How turn ye again to the weak and beggarly elements, under which ye desire again to be in bondage?"

Galatians 4:10 "Ye observe days, and months, and times, and years" even as Armstrong tells his followers to do. For that reason Paul said, "I am afraid I have labored over you in vain."

Galatians 4:21 "Tell me, ye that desire to be under the law, do ye not hear the law?" Then Paul tells of Ishmael, son of the bondwoman, typical of legalists—in contrast to Isaac, son of the free woman who is typical of Christians. Then see what follows—

Galatians 4:30 "Cast out the bondwoman and her son." Cast out OT law! Vs. 31 "We are not children of the bondwoman, but of the free."

Galatians 5:1 "Stand fast, therefore, in the liberty with which Christ hath made us free, and be not entangled again with the yoke of bondage."

Galatians 5:4 "Christ is become of no effect unto you, whosoever of you are justified by the law; ye are fallen from grace." Armstrong does teach salvation by law. Has he not then fallen from grace?

Galatians 5:14 "For all the law is fulfilled in one word, even in this: Thou shalt love thy neighbor as thyself." Then why does HWA use so many unloving words—hate words—against us?

Galatians 5:18 "If ye be led by the Spirit, ye are not under law."

Ephesians 2:15 Christ has "abolished in his flesh the enmity, even the law of commandments contained in ordinances, to make in himself of two one new man, so making peace." How? By breaking down the "middle wall of partition" between Jew-Gentiles and God. When? At the cross when Christ died equally for Jews and Gentiles.

Philippians 3:9 "Not having mine own righteousness, which is of the law, but that which is through the faith of Christ, the righteousness which is of God by faith." Again it is either-or; not both-and.

1 Timothy 1:8, 9 "Knowing this, that the law is not made for a righteous man but for the lawless and disobedient, for the ungodly and for sinners." Rev. D. M. Canright kept the sabbaths 28 years as an Adventist before he saw the gospel truth. Then he wrote that the law was given to Israel only when they became a separate nation; that when Christianity began there was no need for *national* laws since church and state were to be separate, and therefore the Mosaic laws could not apply to Christian people or churches now. This seems to be good, clear thinking.

Titus 3:9 "But avoid . . . strivings about the law; for they are unprofitable and vain." *What good is it* to be bound by inferior OT laws?

Hebrews 7:12 "For the priesthood being changed, there is made of necessity a change also of the law." Isn't this sound logic?

Hebrews 7:18 "For there is verily an annulling of the commandment going before for the weakness and unprofitableness of it."

Hebrews 8:7 "For if that first covenant had been faultless, then should no place have been sought for the second." Then the NT is better!

Hebrews 8:13 "In that he saith, A new covenant, he hath made the first old. Now that which decayeth and groweth old is ready to vanish away." Who prefers a decaying old thing rather than a fresh new one?

Hebrews 10:9 "He taketh away the first, that he may establish the second," referring to the two testaments or covenants.

James 2:10 "For whosoever shall keep the whole law, and yet offend in one point, he is guilty of all." The OT is a long chain of many links, and no Armstrongite knows for sure if he is not breaking some of them.

Revelation 3:9 (also 2:9) "Behold, I will make them of the synagogue of Satan, who say they are Jews, and are not, but do lie. . ." Armstrong has tried hard to make most Englishmen and Americans to be Jews, or Israelites, and thereby place us under obligation to OT laws. We shall treat this matter in chapter 11.

After reading these many verses freeing us from OT laws, it must take a very determined person to follow Armstrong any further. But some people, like the Galatians, are determined; they want to earn merit and a feeling of superiority by being different.

We must therefore continue our analysis of Armstrongism along several interesting lines.

6

WHAT IS THE "HANDWRITING OF ORDINANCES?"

THE ARMSTRONG PEOPLE have published an article with the above title. No author is named. It proposes to show that Colossians 2:14 does not mean the Ten Commandments, but instead they say it is the *record* of our sins. Then let us examine Colossians 8:14–17:

> 14 Blotting out the handwriting of ordinances that was against us, which was contrary to us, and took it out of the way, nailing it to his cross;
> 15 And, having spoiled principalities and powers, he made a show of them openly, triumphing over them in it.
> 16 Let no man, therefore, judge you in food, or in drink, or in respect of a feast day, or of the new moon, or of a sabbath day.
> 17 Which are a shadow of things to come; but the body is of Christ.

We have already shown that 2 Corinthians 3:6-17 tells us that the Old Testament laws were in effect only until Christ came with better laws.

However holy and just and good (Rom. 7:12) the OT law was for the Jews, it is now inferior to the NT laws for all Christians (Heb. 8:6, 13).

"When Christ was crucified, God nailed the Law to His cross," wrote the great NT Greek scholar, Dr. A. T. Robertson (on Col. 2:14).

"In Colossians 2:14 who can fail to see the reference to Sinai in the phrase 'handwriting of ordinances'?" (Dr. A. J. McClain in *Law and Grace*, page 45).

That the "ordinances" of Colossians 2:14 are the Ten Commandments is made sure by the inclusion of "a sabbath day" in verse 16.

The sabbath days, as Jewish feasts and other OT ordinances, were only shadows, "but the body is Christ." Armstrongism tries to sell shadows. Their writers condemn us for honoring the first day of the week. Thereby they violate Colossians 2:16 which forbids such harsh judgments.

And Armstrong has NO proof that the Colossians were sabbatarians, as he alleges.

Neither is there any proof that OT feasts were prescribed to our NT churches. They are mentioned in the Acts and Epistles merely to indicate time. For example, in 1965 my wife and I arrived in Stockholm on Decoration Day, in Paris on our Independence Day, and in Cologne on Bastille Day. In no case did those days demand any recognition from us.

Nor did Christ tell us to observe the Jewish Passover, after the Cross, even though Armstrong says otherwise. To celebrate the Passover now, as Armstrongites do, does not commemorate the death of Christ; it rather denies that He ever died to *fulfill* the Passover typology. And why should Gentiles observe a date meaningful only to Israelites?

In order to change the date of the crucifixion to Wednesday, and the resurrection to Saturday, Armstrong wants to insert an extra "sabbath" into the middle of Passion Week. Yet in this present article, the writer insists that "sabbath days" always mean weekly sabbaths, as in Colossians 2:16.

Now what IS the "handwriting of ordinances?" We do know that the Ten Commandments were the handwriting of God (Exo. 31:18; 32:15, 16), written on hewn stones (Exo. 34:1, 4; Deut. 10:1, 3).

The "ordinances" here *(dogmasin)* are identified in Ephesians 2:15, "Having abolished in his flesh the enmity, even the law of commandments contained in ordinances *(dogmasin)*, to make in himself of two one new man, so making peace." That is, on the cross the OT law was fulfilled and thus abolished; this broke down "the middle wall of partition" between Gentiles,

Jews and God, thus making one new entity—the church (Eph. 2:11–18).

Dr. A. T. Robertson said the "ordinances" of Ephesians 2:15 meant the Mosaic law. Then the same must be true of Colossians 2:14.

"This (Col. 2:14–17) was the law, not in part but in whole— the law in the full compass of its requirements" (P. Fairbairn in *Expositors Greek Testament,* III, 525).

Dr. H. A. Ironside, in his *Lectures on Colossians,* page 91, wrote of "the handwriting of ordinances" that it "could only be properly used of the Ten Commandments, which we are distinctly told were the handwriting of God, embraced in ten ordinances, or divinely-given rules." More, he refers to Colossians 2:16, 17 as "a solemn admonition not to permit ourselves to be disturbed by any who would put us back under the law in any shape or form. . . The very fact that he links the sabbath with the other ceremonies shows clearly that the rule of life for the believer is not the ten words given at Sinai."

But Armstrongism tries to show that Christ died on the cross to free the Colossian people from their previous pagan laws! What a devious detour to avoid the plain truth. And they say it was the *record* of our sins which was nailed to the cross! No; that cheapens the cross.

The Cross meant a great transition from OT law to NT grace. Next.

7

THE NEW TESTAMENT TEACHING ON LAW AND GRACE

ARMSTRONGISM HAS A long article with the above title, written by one W. F. Dankenbring (WFD). He cites Matthew 19:17 where Jesus told a rich young Jewish ruler, "keep the commandments." This statement, WFD says, binds us to the commandments of the OT, including the Saturday-Sabbath, the seventh day of the week.

But this command was given to a Jew, not a Gentile. And it was given before the death and resurrection of Christ, during the transition between the coming of John the Baptist with the NT gospel and the completion of Christ's work on earth. Also, it was a device of a teacher in suggesting further thinking by his pupil.

A relevant verse here is John 1:17, "For the law was given by Moses, but grace and truth came by Jesus Christ." This verse surely says that the law of Moses was superseded by God's higher plan of grace and truth. The transition time is further indicated in Mark 1:1; Luke 16:16; Acts 10:37 and 13:24.

Contrary to WFD, the higher principles and standards of the NT are quite as strong against idolatry, cursing, murder, stealing, lust, lying, cheating, etc., as the Mosaic laws ever were. So—we are not antinomians; that is, we are not lawless. And what is the harm in observing Sundays?

Armstrong cites Psalm 111:7, 8 as saying that the commandments stand fast for ever. But elsewhere he admits that "forever" sometimes means "for an age," or during a certain era. This is true. More, God has many commandments other than the ten given to Moses in Sinai. He has certain laws which people from Adam to Moses knew, and which are eternal, for they are not confined to any one dispensation.

Mr. WFD implies that those who disagree with him thereby accuse God of being fickle. Not so; but we do believe that He gave us the NT with its higher standards as a replacement of the OT Jewish laws.

And WFD asks what is wrong with the OT laws? Well, "the law made nothing perfect, but the bringing in of a better hope did" (Heb. 7:19). "For the law, having a shadow of good things to come and not the very image of those things, can never . . . make those who come to it perfect. . . . For by one offering he (Christ) hath perfected forever them that are sanctified" (Heb. 10:1, 14).

Then Mr. WFD accuses God of creating us with a carnal, defiant, and rebellious nature. We disagree. After God made man He called all His creation "very good" (Gen. 1:29). It was the devil who put evil in man.

Then WFD plays a trick with words, this time with "end" which is in Romans 10:4 and James 5:11. He should know that in James the word is an obsolete English usage, as in an old catechism—"What is the chief *end* of man?" Answer: "Man's chief *end* is to glorify God and to enjoy Him forever." The word here means purpose, or aim. But in Romans 10:4 the word means culmination, terminus, or destination. "For Christ is the end of the law for righteousness to every one that believeth." That is, we who believe in Christ find full salvation in Him alone, and not in any law.

On Romans 10:4 Dr. A. T. Robertson wrote, "Christ put a stop to the law as a means of salvation (Rom. 6:14; Eph. 2:15; Col. 2:14), as in Luke 16:16. Christ is the goal of the law (Gal. 3:24). Christ is the fulfillment of the law (Matt. 5:17; Rom. 13:10; 1 Tim. 1:5). Christ ended the law as a method of salvation for all who believe, Jew or Gentile. Christ wrote *finis* on the law as a means of grace" (*Word pictures*, 387, 388).

WFD stumbles badly in his "exposition" of Romans 7:4, 6. He says "delivered from the law" means only deliverance from its death penalty, but verse 6 does not say that. It DOES free us from the OT law: "But now we are delivered from the law, that being dead in which we were held, that we should serve in newness of spirit and not in the oldness of the letter."

WFD has still more trouble with Romans 6:14, "for ye are not under the law, but under grace." This agrees perfectly with John 1:17, for we are now in the NT era. The Book of Galatians explains that it is now law OR grace. It cannot be both law AND grace at the same time (Gal. 5:1-4).

Again Armstrongism tries to frighten us into believing his violations of grammar and his bad exegesis. He threatens us with the lake of fire if we do not conform to his Jewish-law bondage.

* * *

"Which Old Testament Laws Should We Keep Today?" is an article by Mr. H. L. Hoeh, an Armstrong senior editor. He agrees with WFD. Mr. Hoeh tries to show that one's character depends on knowing the difference between the moral laws and the ceremonial laws of the OT. But nowhere in the Bible is such a distinction made. The Bible *never* speaks of one law as "moral" and another as "ceremonial." James 2:10 says the OT laws are like a chain; break one and you break them all.

Mr. Hoeh mistakenly says that Abraham had the Ten Commandments, but Nehemiah 9:14 says they were not made known until the time of Moses. "The Lord made *not* this covenant (Ten Commandments) with our fathers, but with us, even us, who are all of us here alive this day" (Deut. 5:3). Then Moses repeated the Decalogue. See also John 1:17; 7:19.

And Armstrongism wants us to observe the annual Passovers now, even though Christ fulfilled their prophetic typology fully. They were only "shadows" of the realities to follow (Col. 2:17; Heb. 10:1). We now have Christ who is the reality. So—who needs shadows? Yes, we can study the shadows for they teach us about Christ. Only yesterday, as I now write, did some former church members of mine tell me gratefully of the helps my sermons on the OT tabernacle were to them 32 years before. I had a model of the tabernacle and its furniture, and gave one sermon to each part of the OT rituals, showing how each one foreshadowed Christ.

Mr. Hoeh tries to evade circumcision by separating Mosaic laws into moral and ceremonial divisions. But he has no verse to authorize such a division. No such verse can be found.

On the other hand, Acts 15 tells about the Jerusalem church

council where the OT laws and ceremonies were discussed. The apostles and elders, "with the whole church" (vs. 22, 28, 29), declared that "it seemed good to the Holy Spirit, and to us, to lay upon you no greater burden than these necessary things: That ye abstain from things offered to idols, and from blood, and from things strangled, and from fornication. . ." Then, they need NOT "keep the law" (v. 24). This glorious liberty is still ours, in spite of Armstrong's persistent propaganda.

This decision made it official. The OT laws were no longer binding. The OT feast days and sabbaths were obsolete. The Lord's Day outshines all OT holy days as the sun outshines millions of stars.

Let us then examine just how our NT Sundays are now superior to Saturdays as rest-and-worship days for all informed Christians. This Sabbath question is vital to Armstrongism; it is their keystone. If it falls, their entire structure collapses.

8

REASONS FOR HONORING SUNDAY OVER SABBATH

Sunday, the first day of the week, commemorates the greatest fact in history, the resurrection of our Lord and Savior Jesus Christ. And the day before His resurrection was surely the saddest day for Christians.

The Lord's Day vs The Grief Day

In all history, which day could be called the most fittingly "The Day of Grief?" Would it not be the one full day when the devil had Christ in the grave? For that was a day of anguish, distress, and extreme sorrow.

When Jesus faced His deadly foes in Gethsemane, where Judas betrayed Him, He said to them, "This is your hour, and the power of darkness." Or, "This is your moment—the time when Satan's power reigns supreme" (Luke 22:53). Of course God is always supreme, but on that Saturday He let the devil have his day.

From that moment until Christ arose, including all day Saturday, *the devil had his day!* He had "the power of death" (Heb. 2:14) on that sad sabbath day.

Christ was crucified and buried on a Friday. Six times that day is called the "preparation" day (paraskeue, Greek; Matt. 27:62; Mark 15:42; Luke 23:54; John 19:14, 31, 42). Modern Greeks still use that same word for Friday. The Jews used Fridays in preparation for their sabbaths. (All honor to the

55

Old Testament sabbaths—in the *Old* dispensation. But now sabbath-keepers dishonor the Lord's Day, our glorious day of worship in the New Testament dispensation.)

Christ in the grave on that sabbath symbolizes the death of OT sacrifices, ordinances, and laws (Eph. 2:15, 16; Col. 2:14–17).

That awful Saturday of Christ's burial was the devil's day of triumph.

1. Then he had Christ dead with a spear-pierced heart, locked in a grave with a boulder, sealed by Imperial Rome, guarded by soldiers (Matt. 27:60–66). No; God was not defeated or surprised; He was in control, but He allowed Satan to have that Saturday of temporary victory.

2. On that awful sabbath, Satan had chief priests and Pharisees calling Christ "a deceiver" (Matt. 27:63).

3. On that sabbath, Satan had Pilate say about Christ's tomb, "Make it as sure as you can" (Matt. 27:65). It was a tomb-gloom day.

4. On that sabbath, evil men wished to make Christ a liar (Matt. 27:63).

5. On the sabbath, the devil would make sure no thieves could steal Christ's body (Matt. 27:64). But on that sad day the disciples were timid.

6. On the sabbath, evil men suspected Christ's disciples would lie about Him (Matt. 27:64). That dreadful Saturday was NOT the Lord's Day.

7. On that sabbath, all Christ's *enemies* rejoiced over His *dead* body—

    a. The mob that had shouted, "Crucify Him!" (Mark. 15:13).

    b. Those Jews who had tried to stone Him (John 10:31, 39).

    c. The wicked Jews who said He blasphemed (John 10:33).

    d. The priests and Pharisees who wanted to kill Him (John 11:47–53, 57).

    e. The Pharisees who said He did the devil's work (Matt. 12:14).

    f. The false witnesses who lied against Him (Matt. 26:59–61).

g. All the demons who hated Him, then and now (Matt. 8:28, 29).

8. But Christ's *friends* were in great grief on that sabbath day—

a. They did not expect Him to rise again (John 20: 2, 9, 11, 13, 25).

b. They planned to honor His *dead body* (Mark 16:1; Luke 23:56; 24:1).

c. The women rested that day, according to the commandment (Luke 23:56).

d. There was no preaching of any Good News on that sabbath!

e. On that sabbath, no one saw or heard Christ; no Christian rejoiced, and *no one* worshiped Him. But they all did on the next day—SUNDAY!

If you had been there then, which day would you celebrate?

The New Life Day vs The Old Law Day

The supreme task of the early Christians was witnessing to the Resurrection of our Lord Jesus Christ. It should be so now as well.

On that First Day of the week, Sunday, believers witnessed that Christ had defeated the devil and his followers. And they kept at it!

Acts 1:22 The 12th official witness of His resurrection was ordained.

Acts 2:32 "This Jesus hath God raised up, whereof we all are witnesses."

Acts 3:15 "whom God hath raised from the dead, of which we are witnesses."

Acts 4:33 "with *great power* gave the apostles witness of the resurrection."

Acts 5:31 "Him hath God exalted . . . and we are witnesses of these things."

1 Cor. 15:14 "If Christ be not risen our preaching . . . your faith is vain."

What fact in the Bible is more important than Christ's resurrection? What event in the NT is emphasized more, or is more basic to our faith?

What day of the week witnesses to His resurrection better than Sunday?

What day of the week was more hopeless for Christians than Saturday?

What day best honors the "New Creation" or the NT Gospel (2 Cor. 5:17)?

"This is the day the Lord hath made; we will rejoice and be glad in it."

Christ's deadly foes celebrated Saturday. Christ-hating Jews still do. But Christ and hundreds of millions of Christians glorify The Lord's Day.

Christ repeatedly prophesied His death—and rising again "the third day." The third day from Friday (preparation) would be Sunday, according to examples of Jewish reckoning in Luke 13:32; 1 Samuel 20:12 and Acts 27:18, 19. So, Christ "rose again the third day according to the Scriptures" (1 Cor. 15:4). This was a Sunday, our Sunday.

Christ Glorifies Sundays as Better Days

Since Christ is Lord of the Sabbath (Mark 2:28), He has authority to change it for a better day. He did bring in many "better" things than the OT ever had. "Better" is *kreisson* (Greek), meaning more powerful.

Hebrews 1:4 Christ is "so much better than the angels."

Hebrews 6:9 "better things" are expected of NT Christians.

Hebrews 7:19 "the law (OT) made nothing perfect" but "a better hope did"

Hebrews 7:22 "Jesus was made a surety of a better covenant"

Hebrews 8:6 Christ gave us "a more excellent ministry" and "a better covenant" which is "established upon better promises."

Hebrews 9:23 NT Christians have "better sacrifices" than those in the OT.

Hebrews 12:24 Jesus and the NEW covenant have "better things."

The New Day vs The Jew Day

Mark 2:27 "The sabbath was made for man, and not man for the sabbath."

Then—man is more important than the sabbath

And—the OT sabbath could be changed or displaced by a day far better

So—the OT sabbaths ended when Christ rose from the dead, as we read in—

Matthew 28:1 "In the end of the sabbaths" (*sabbaton*, Greek plural)

Matthew 28:2 God honored Sunday with "a great earthquake" and by sending His angel to roll back the stone. The angel then sat upon the stone, picturing the NT conquest of OT bonds, of our foes, and of our sins.

Matthew 28:3 "raiment white as snow" symbolizes "the righteousness of saints" (Rev. 3:4, 5; 19:8), secured by Christ's resurrection triumph.

Matthew 28:5, 6 Christ's resurrection was physical and very real.

Matthew 28:7 Spread the Good News! Tell it and preach it on Sundays!

Matthew 28:8 Christians had "great joy" on Sunday.

Matthew 28:9 *Christians worshiped their Lord on Sunday!* Why not now also? They told, by teaching and preaching, the Good News on Sunday. Jesus commanded them on Sunday. "Rejoice!" (*Chairete*, Matt. 28:9).

Matthew 28:10 Jesus directed believers to tell the Good News on Sunday.

Matthew 28:11-15 Christ's foes lied, paid bribes, to deny this Sunday Gospel, but Rome's mighty power was defeated on Sunday.

The Good News Day vs The Bad News Day

Mark 16:2 The first Easter Sunrise Service, a good example for us now. (The name "Easter" was not Christian, but *now* it has been Christianized by good gospel churches—another Christian victory over paganism.)

Mark 16:7 Tell the Good News, on Sunday.

Mark 16:8 This Sunday miracle amazed these three Christians.

Mark 16:9 "Jesus had risen early on the first day of the week".

Mark 16:10 Mary Magdalene told the Good News on Sunday.

Mark 16:11, 13 This great Sunday news was incredible—at first.

Mark 16:14 Jesus rebuked those Sunday doubters.

The Life Day vs The Death Day

Luke 24:5 "Why seek ye the living (Christ) among the dead?" (among dead OT laws, sacrifices, ordinances, and feasts?)

Luke 24:9, 10 The Gospel was preached on Sunday, and all Sundays since then.

Luke 24:17-32 Jesus preached the Gospel on Sunday.

Luke 24:25 Many important prophecies were fulfilled on this Sunday.

Luke 24:26 Christ entered into His glory on Sunday.

Luke 24:32 Christ "opened the Scriptures" on Sunday.

Luke 24:36 Jesus declared "Peace be unto you" on Sunday.

Luke 24:44-48 Again, Jesus preached the Gospel on Sunday.

Luke 24:48 The disciples witnessed to these great Sunday events.

The Worship Day vs The Worry Day

John 20:1 "The first day of the week"—Sunday—is glorified repeatedly.

John 20:2 Mary Magdalene RAN with Sunday's spectacular news.

John 20:4 Peter and John RAN on Sunday to verify the wonderful news.

John 20:11-18 Weeping was changed to rejoicing on this Sunday.

John 20:17 Jesus commanded the Good News to be proclaimed on Sunday.

John 20:19 Jesus met His disciples on Sunday and blessed them.

John 20:20 "Then were the disciples glad when they saw the Lord."

John 20:21 Jesus commissioned His disciples on Sunday.

John 20:22 Jesus gave the Holy Spirit to His disciples on Sunday.

John 20:23 Jesus gave His people gospel authority on Sunday.

John 20:24, 25 Thomas wanted proof of Sunday's incredible news. He had refused, or neglected, to meet with other disciples the Sunday before.

John 20:26 Jesus met His disciples on the second Sunday (not sabbath!)

John 20:28 Thomas finally believed, and worshiped Christ on Sunday.

John 20:29 Jesus blesses us who now believe in Sunday's Good News. We wish all Armstrongites would believe these great verses.

The Church Day vs The Jewish Day

Acts 2:1 "the day of Pentecost was fully come"—Sunday (Lev. 23:16).

Acts 2:4 The Holy Spirit honored Sunday by filling Christian worshipers.

Acts 2:17 God the Father honored this Sunday by giving His Spirit then.

Acts 2:4-11 The Christians preached the Gospel on this Sunday.

Acts 2:14-40 Peter preached the Good News on this Sunday.

Acts 2:41 Christ honored this Sunday by saving 3,000 people who believed.

On this Sunday, 3,000 converts were baptized

On this Sunday, 3,000 converts were added to the church

Acts 2:32, 33 Father, Son, and Holy Spirit glorified this Sunday. Who, then, one week or two weeks or ten weeks later, would forsake Sundays for Saturdays? Unthinkable! Sundays had most divine meaning and importance.

Acts 20:6, 7 25 years later, Christians met on Sundays for worship, preaching, and the Lord's Supper—after six days (including Saturday) without such worship there at Troas.

The Meeting Day vs The Mourning Day

On Sundays, the Corinthian Christians had collections (1 Cor. 16:1, 2). These were customary parts of meetings for worship there, as in Galatia, "with all that in *every place* call upon the name of Jesus Christ" (1 Cor. 1:2). Thus, officially, Sundays were the days for Christian worship everywhere.

But in order to reach the many unconverted Jews, they would preach on sabbath days also. After the Resurrection, whenever Christians met by themselves, it was on Sundays. This was the day Christ glorified.

Sunday is "the day which the Lord hath made" (Psalm 118:22-24), identified in Acts 4:10-12 as Sunday, the day of Christ's

Resurrection. Therefore, it is "THE LORD'S DAY" of Revelation 1:10. What more proof is needed? So we worship on that glad day. We "rejoice and are glad" on Sundays.

We can follow the examples of Christ, Peter, John, and Paul, with all other NT Christians who met on the Lord's Day for worship, preaching, and for collections.

What day in all the world's history is greater than the Sunday of Christ's Resurrection victory and triumph? On what day but Sunday have greater prophecies been fulfilled? or more hopes realized? On what other day can all the world look for such rich meanings?

The Master's Day vs Moses' Day

The OT sabbaths were for Israelites only (Exo. 20:2, 12; 31: 13-17; Deut. 5:1-15; Neh. 9:14; Ezek. 20:12, 20; Rom. 2:14, etc.). Never is any Gentile, or Hebrew-Christian, told to keep OT sabbaths or feasts. We are not Jews (Rev. 2:9; 3:9), in spite of what Armstrongism says.

The OT Feast of First Fruits was on a Sunday, "the day after the sabbath," and it prophesied Christ's resurrection (Lev. 23:11; 1 Cor. 15:20-23).

The OT Feast of Wave Loaves was on a Sunday, "the day after the sabbath," and it prophesied Pentecost (Lev. 23:15-21; Acts 2:1).

Among the many duties prescribed, and sins rebuked, in the NT—no mention of any sabbath law is ever included. This is significant.

The OT sabbaths and feasts were merely "shadows" of better NT days (Col. 2:16, 17; Heb. 8:5; 10:1). Who wants to live on shadows?

The last sabbath mentioned in the Bible is in Acts 18:4, at Corinth where Paul later wrote of collections "on the first day of the week," a clear change from OT sabbaths to NT Sundays. Colossians 2:16 agrees.

The "Supreme Court" of the early churches, the "apostles and elders" in Jerusalem, assured ALL Christians that the OT laws of Moses (Acts 15:5, 19, 24, 28, 29) were not binding on any Christians, Jews or Gentiles.

The NT laws and commandments (1 John 2:3-8; 3:4; 22-24; 4:21; 5:2, 3) were different from, and superior to, the OT laws.

Why have a NEW Testament at all if it is not to be received and enjoyed in place of the old?

Christopher Wordsworth wrote lovely lines about our Sundays—

> On thee, at the creation,
>   The light first had its birth;
> On thee, for our salvation,
>   Christ rose from depths of earth;
> On thee our Lord victorious
>   The Spirit sent from heaven;
> And thus on thee most glorious
>   A triple light was given.
>
>   *   *   *

I have asked many Seventh Day Adventists and Armstrong people to cite one Bible verse that commands a Gentile to keep any Saturday-Sabbath. Not one person has ever yet found such a verse. This fatal flaw invalidates their entire system. The best that the Armstrong headquarters could give me on this question was Galatians 3:28, 29 and Hebrews 4:9; neither passage tells any Gentile to keep any sabbath!

Dr. M. F. Unger wrote, "This fourth commandment, it must be emphasized, was never imposed upon any nation or people except Israel . . . Nowhere is sabbath keeping ever imposed upon a Christian in this age of grace. Indeed, the very opposite is true" (*Bibliotheca Sacra,* Jan.-Mar., 1966, p. 56, 57).

This OT sabbath law says, "Six days shalt thou labor, and do *all* thy work" (Exo. 20:9). Yet H. W. Armstrong wrote 9-26-71 that his son Garner Ted was working "DAILY—seven days a week . . . He is forced to go at high tension . . ." How many Armstrongites work six days each week, or seven, or five, or none?

Those who keep sabbaths thereby substitute law for grace, Moses for Christ, works for faith, earth for heaven, the old creation for the new, and a dead Christ for our living Christ. It is as though Christ is still in the grave, and that He died in vain (Gal. 2:21).

It was said of Jesus, "What evil hath he done" (Luke 23:22). So we ask, "What evil has Sunday worship ever done?" What man, or church, or nation has ever been made worse by it? But Armstrongism says it means we are sun-worshipers and Satan-worshipers because of it! They ought to rejoice, instead, that Sunday-keepers have completely defeated sun worship in all civilized lands. But Armstrong's attacks would have his imaginary sun-god powerful enough to control the rest day for one billion people all over the world. Fantastic.

An Armstrong tract asks, "Which Day is the Sabbath of the New Testament?" We answer that the OT sabbath was observed until the resurrection; thereafter many Christians observed both the seventh and first days for a time, but soon they kept the first day exclusively. John 5:17, 18 seems to say that Christ broke the sabbath!

This tract, pages 10 to 12, dares to say that Acts 20:1-7 does not describe a Sunday meeting! But it does: "upon the *first day* of the week, when the disciples came together to break bread, Paul preached unto them . . ." To "break bread" means the Lord's Supper as in 1 Corinthians 10:16; 11:24. Armstrong says it was an ordinary meal, but that would mean they had not eaten for seven days! This tract, on pages 15 and 16, also tries to evade Sunday collections in 1 Corinthians 16:1, 2. It says that it was not money, but *fruit*, that was to be collected and carried to the poor in Jerusalem! He quotes Romans 15:25-28 where "fruit" is used figuratively, not literally. The same is true in Romans 1:13 and 6:21, 22.

✿   ✿   ✿

The early Christians observed Sundays as their holy days.

Ignatius, Bishop of Antioch, 110 A.D., wrote, ". . . no longer observing the Sabbath, but fashioning their lives after the Lord's Day on which our life also arose through Him, that we may be found disciples of Christ."

Justin Martyr, 100-165: "And on the day called Sunday, all who live in cities or in the country gather together . . . Sunday is the day on which we all hold our solemn assembly because it is the first day on which God, having wrought a change in the darkness of matter, made the world; and Jesus Christ our Savior on the same day rose from the dead."

The Epistle of Barnabas, 120-150: ". . . we keep the eighth day with joyfulness, a day also in which Jesus rose from the dead."

Irenaeus, 178: "The mystery of the Lord's resurrection may not be celebrated on any other day than the Lord's Day."

Bardaisan, born 154: ". . . upon one day which is the first day of the week we assemble ourselves together . . ."

Cyprian, 200-258: "The Lord's Day is both the first and eighth day."

Eusebius, 315: ". . . the Lord's resurrection should be celebrated on no other day than the Lord's Day."

Peter, Bishop of Alexandria, 300: "We keep the Lord's Day as a day of joy because of Him who arose thereon."

"Thus it appears that from apostolic times, the Christian churches observed the Lord's Day or the first day of the week; further, the Jewish Sabbath, in the words of Clement of Alexandria (about 194) was 'nothing more than a working day.' " (from Walter R. Martin, *The Kingdom of the Cults,* 395, 396. Bethany Fellowship, Inc., Minneapolis, Minn.)

We believe that many sabbatarians are saved, not because of sabbath-keeping, but in spite of it. And we would really like for everyone to enjoy the supreme joys of Easter. To that greatest of happy Sundays we now give our attention.

9

THE PLAIN TRUTH
ABOUT EASTER

Mr. HERBERT W. ARMSTRONG (HWA) keeps going around and around the Old Testament laws which have been supplanted by the higher New Testament laws (2 Cor. 3:6-17). His writers follow him. "But their minds were blinded; for until this day remaineth the same veil untaken away in the reading of the old testament; which veil is done away in Christ" (v. 14).

Why are Armstrongites blinded? One clue is the recent "God is dead" blasphemy of a few liberals. Armstrong writers have "killed" the Holy Spirit. They destroyed—for themselves—the Personality of the Holy Spirit by downgrading Him to a "force," or an "it." How, then, can they ever know *what the Spirit says* in the Bible?

"But the natural man receiveth not the things of the Spirit of God; for they are foolishness unto him, neither can he know them because they are spiritually discerned" (1 Cor. 2:14). "These are they who separate themselves, sensual, *having not the Spirit*" (Jude 19). Assuredly, the Armstrongites are "scoffers" (Jude 19); they also "set up divisions" and by their own writings have divested themselves of the Person of the Holy Spirit. The word "sensual" is found only in Jude 19 and James 3:15 where it reads, "This wisdom descendeth not from above, but is earthly, sensual, demoniacal."

Armstrong insists that Christ had to be in the grave full 72 hours in order to validate Matthew 12:40. And he insists, contrary to Seventh Day Adventists, that Christ was crucified on a Wednesday and arose on a Saturday. Their aim seems to be to demolish our happy Easter days, in addition to destroying all our Sundays each year. Is this part of their psychological strategy in making themselves out to be wiser and superior to 99% of the world's Christian people?

Jesus told His disciples repeatedly that He would be killed, and then raised again the third day (Matt. 16:21 and 13 other places; "three days" is used nine times for Christ's entombment). HWA insists that this means a full 72 hours; better scholars know that Jewish reckoning was not like ours in this mechanistic, assembly-line, clock-watching age.

For the Biblical use of "the third day" see 1 Samuel 20:12, "O Lord God of Israel, when I have sounded my father about to-morrow any time, or the third day . . ." So—the day after to-morrow is the third day!

"And he (Jesus) said unto them, Go, and tell that fox, Behold, I cast out demons, and I do cures today and tomorrow, and the third day I shall have finished" (Luke 13:32). So Jesus Himself told us what the third day meant; it meant the day after to-morrow. Thus, from the Friday of crucifixion, the day after to-morrow would be Sunday, the third day.

"And we being exceedingly tossed with a tempest, the next day they lightened the ship; and *the third day* we cast out with our own hands the tackle of the ship" (Acts 27:18, 19).

Dr. Alfred Edersheim, a very learned Jewish-Christian scholar, in Volume II, *Life and Times of Jesus the Messiah*, p. 630, 631 —"It was the *first day of the week,* according to Jewish reckoning the third day from His death." (His footnote on this: "Friday, Saturday, Sunday.")

Dr. A. T. Robertson, famous NT Greek scholar, wrote on Mark 16:2—

> The body of Jesus was buried late on Friday before the sabbath (our Saturday) which began at sunset. This is made clear as a bell by Luke 23:54 "And the sabbath drew on." The women rested on the sabbath (Luke 23:56). This visit of the women was in the early morning of our Sunday, the first day of the week.
> Some people are greatly disturbed over the fact that Jesus did not remain in the grave full 72 hours. But He repeatedly said that He would rise on the third day and that is precisely what

happened. He was buried on Friday afternoon. He was risen on Sunday morning. If He had really remained in the tomb full three days and then had risen after that, it would have been the fourth day, not the third day. The occasional phrase, "after three days," is merely a vernacular idiom common in all languages and not meant to be exact and precise like "on the third day." (*Word Pictures in the New Testament*, I, 399, 400).

Dr. George W. Clark, another thorough NT scholar, on Mark 16:2—

The first day of the week. Sunday, the Lord's Day (Rev. 1:10). This day, on which Jesus rose from the dead, was ever afterwards observed by the disciples as the day of Christian rest. And how appropriately! If the day when God rested from the work of creation was hallowed and observed, *how much more* the day when Christ rested from the *greater work* of redemption!

It was fitting that that day of unparalleled darkness, when Jesus lay in the grave, should be the last of Jewish sabbaths, and that the birthday of immortality and of Christ's finished work should ever after be the day of the Christian's rest. . . . (*Notes on Mark*, p. 316, 317).

Justin Martyr wrote that keeping Sunday was a matter of life or death for the early Christians. If one confessed to keeping Sunday, he would be killed or tortured or both. If he failed to keep Sunday, or if he denied it, then he might live on. Since the early martyrs paid such a price for our Sundays, we ought to value them more than we do.

✿   ✿   ✿

The connection between our first-day Sundays and first-day Easters is obvious. The Bible supports both; Armstrongism denies both.

Mr. HWA makes a big deal about the alleged origin of the word "Easter." His references to "Ishtar" are far fetched and beside the point. His smoke screen is irrelevant. One could write much about the heathenism back of the names of the week like Wednesday, Thursday, Friday, and Saturday. Do we Christians become heathenish because we use these names? Of course not! Yet HWA accuses us of devil-worship because we honor Sundays and Easters. He ought to rejoice with us, instead, that our Christ has prevailed over "Ishtar" and the many other pagan gods of antiquity.

Consider the vast worldwide testimony to our risen Christ in each observance of Easter. Quite apart from immaterial accretions like eggs, rabbits, and hot cross buns, the vast majority of evangelical Christians celebrate the day commendably. The name "Easter" has become Christianized; only Armstrongites wish to degrade it and debase it and slander it with their diatribes on its heathen origin.

Many Christians like to buy new clothes before Easter. What better time? This is not personal vanity; it is a desire to honor Christ's great day with one's very best appearance. We wear our best clothes for honored guests, or hosts; why not honor our Lord as much?

Even the earth's northern hemisphere dresses up in new and beautiful foliage during the Easter season. And what is more beautiful than Easter lilies? With them we honor the Christ of the resurrection who is Himself clothed in white garments (Matt. 17:2). And He has promised that we who trust Him and obey Him shall also one day be clothed in white—"fine linen, clean and white; for the fine linen is the righteousness of the saints" (Rev. 19:8). Our churches do their very best for Christ on Easter days.

But Armstrongism tries to besmirch with heathenism all that is connected with our glorious Easter celebrations. Why does he want to do·that?

Then Mr. HWA says the whole world, except himself, has been deceived about Easter. This is much like the one straying sheep declaring that the other 99 were all ignorant, lost, misled, and deceived!

As for those who attend Easter sunrise services, Armstrong says we thereby worship the sun-god, and he calls this abominable idolatry. But Christ's most devoted followers went at sunrise to see what they supposed was Christ's dead body in the grave; how much more should we honor the living Christ on Easter morning?

❂   ❂   ❂

Mr. Armstrong wrote more against Easter in a tract, "The Resurrection Was Not on Sunday." He repeats the 72-hour idea, saying it is the only sign that Christ was the Messiah. Again he is badly wrong; every miracle Christ did, and the words He spoke, all testify to His Messiahship.

And 72 hours were not needed to prove that Christ had really died. His side was pierced with a spear so that His blood ran out; everyone knew His body was totally dead; and the grave clothes were wrapped entirely around His head and body. So, whether His body was in the tomb 72 hours or 32 hours would not affect the reality of His resurrection.

HWA is wrong again in saying that Genesis 1:4-13 is the only place where the Bible explains the phrase, "the third day." Let him ponder 1 Samuel 20:12; Luke 13:32 and Acts 27:18, 19; these should show him the truth.

During all of that Saturday-Sabbath, Christ's foes rejoiced, for they knew they had finally killed Him. On the other hand, His friends were in tomb-gloom despair on that saddest of all days. Their grief was abysmal.

Came the dawn! The First Day of the week! Sunday! Easter! Real joy! Christ's friends rejoiced exceedingly, then and ever since. But Christ's foes—on that epochal Sunday—were all defeated, disgraced, desperate, discredited, dishonored, and shamed.

Until this good hour, every Bible-loving Christian has rejoiced over each Sunday, and even more over each Easter, because they remind us so beautifully of Christ's greatest victory.

> Christ, the Lord, is ris'n today; Hallelujah!
> Sons of men and angels say: Hallelujah!
> Raise your joys and triumphs high; Hallelujah!
> Sing, ye heav'ns, and, earth, reply. Hallelujah!
>
> Love's redeeming work is done, Hallelujah!
> Fought the fight, the battle won: Hallelujah!
> Lo! our Son's eclipse is o'er; Hallelujah!
> Lo! He sets in blood no more. Hallelujah!
>
> Vain the stone, the watch, the seal, Hallelujah!
> Christ hath burst the gates of hell: Hallelujah!
> Death in vain forbids His rise, Hallelujah!
> Christ hath opened paradise. Hallelujah!
> —Charles Wesley

❊   ❊   ❊

Since HWA keeps on insisting that Christ was crucified on a Wednesday, let us take a look at the record.

10

ARMSTRONG DENIES FRIDAY CRUCIFIXION

My NON-ARMSTRONG friends who believe in a Wednesday or Thursday crucifixion day will please bear with me here. I respect their views as genuine Christian brethren. But I disapprove of Armstrong's writers whose main purpose seems to be to attack all of Christendom.

In Armstrong's efforts to discredit our Sundays, he insists on Saturday as the day of Christ's resurrection. Then in order to make room for his 72-hour entombment of Christ, he must have the crucifixion on Wednesday.

Mr. Herman L. Hoeh, now Armstrong's executive editor, has two tracts: "The Crucifixion Was not on Friday" and "How to Prove the Crucifixion Was not on Friday." He rashly asserts that if our Good Friday-Easter belief is true, then we have no Savior. He uses baseless reasoning so often.

Mr. Hoeh depends too much on his faulty reading of John 19:14. "And it was the preparation of the passover . . ." Dr. A. T. Robertson on this—

> The preparation of the passover (*paraskeue tou pascha*). That is, Friday of passover week, the preparation day before the sabbath of passover week (or feast). See also verses 31, 42; Mark 15:24; Matt. 27:62; Luke 23:54 for this same use of *paraskeue* for Friday. It is the name for Friday today in Greece (*Word Pictures in the New Testament*, V, 299).

On Matthew 27:62—"the day of the preparation"—Dr. Robert-

71

son commented, *"Paraskeue* is the name in modern Greek for Friday." I checked this with a man from Greece, and he agreed.

Dr. George W. Clark commented on Mark 15:42, "and now when the evening was come, because it was the preparation, that is, the day before the sabbath,"

> As the Jewish sabbath was Saturday, the *preparation* was Friday. Such is the use of the term in Matthew 27:62; Luke 23: 54; John 19:31, 42. From Josephus we learn that the preparation was strictly Friday afternoon from three o'clock until sunset (*Antiquities* xvi, 6, 2); but in popular usage it was applied to Friday, and is so translated in the Syriac. The *Preparation* is the name by which Friday is now generally known in Asia and Greece. *(Notes on Mark,* 309).
>
> Dr. Clark on Luke 23:54—The preparation was Friday the day before the Jewish sabbath, which was Saturday; the day for making ready for the sabbath. And on John 19:14—This is the most important mark of time; it fixes the day of our Lord's crucifixion as Friday, 15th Nisan, the first day of the passover festival. It shows that Jesus and the disciples ate the passover at the right time, the evening of 14th Nisan.
>
> Dr. Clark on John 19:24—This memorable day was Friday. And on Mark 15:47—The Jewish mode of reckoning a portion of a day as the whole has long been understood and acknowledged (1 Sam. 30:1, 12; Esther 4:16; 5:1; Hosea 6:2). Josephus frequently reckons the extreme portions of two years as two years. The objection that Jesus would not have been "three days" in the grave shows a want of familiarity with Hebrew usage. . . . To suppose it not a regular sabbath, but merely a ceremonial one, is forced and unnatural. . . . There is no clear proof that there was a special preparation day for the Passover.

Alfred Edersheim, the great Jewish-Christian scholar, also contradicts Armstrong on such matters relating to Jewish times and dates.

And Alexander Cruden, in his helpful concordance notes, wrote—

> The Jews gave the name of *Paraskeue* to the sixth day (Friday) of the week, because being not allowed on the sabbath to prepare their food, they provided the day before what was necessary for their subsistence on the sabbath. John 19:14 says that Friday, on which our Savior suffered, was the preparation of the passover, because the passover was to be celebrated the day following. St. Matthew marks out the day by these words, "The day that followed the day of the preparation" (Matt. 27:62, Saturday).

Mr. Hoeh blames the apostolic fathers, those faithful and intelligent Christians who wrote during the first Christian centuries, for justifying an alleged pagan tradition to connect the Sunday-resurrection with Nimrod! Utterly incredible! We know that the apostolic fathers were very careful to keep ALL paganism out of Christianity. They suffered terrible tortures rather than compromise with paganism. Mr. Hoeh should apologize to them.

Mr. Hoeh tries to show that Christ died on Wednesday, the middle day of the week, because Daniel 9:27 has such a phrase. ". . . in the midst of the week he shall cause the sacrifice and the oblation to cease . . ." But this suggests the exact opposite of Mr. Hoeh's assumption!

Mr. Hoeh writes at great length on his notions of ancient Hebrew calendars. He says that God at first divided an hour into 1080 parts(!), with each part being three and one-third seconds! Incredible. But Mr. Hoeh wrote five big pages of obfuscating figures involving seconds, minutes, hours, new moons, feasts, variable years, varying calendars—all evidently meant to impress readers with sheer quantity. It is not Biblical.

A Seventh-Day Adventist, R. L. Odom, says that not one Bible text shows that Jesus rose on Saturday. He quoted the *Jewish Encyclopedia*—"In Jewish communal life, part of a day is at times reckoned as one day . . . In religious practices a part of a day is sometimes counted as a full day." Of all people, the Seventh-Day Adventists would like to honor Saturdays but they refuse to twist the Bible on this matter.

The Jews used "inclusive reckoning" as in 2 Kings 18:9, 10 for "three years" whereas our "western" culture would say two years.

Matthew 28:1-15 says the guardsmen at Christ's grave were still on duty Sunday morning. *While* the women (vss. 1, 7-10) "were going" (v. 11) from the tomb, the guards "came into the city." The "great earthquake" (v. 2) occurred in connection with an angel opening the tomb and the risen Christ arising—all very early on "the first day of the week." (See our chapter 8). Now if Christ had risen on Saturday, as Mr. Hoeh says, the guards would have known it and so would everyone else.

To insist on a literal 72-hour burial should mean equal insistence on Christ's body being "in the heart of the earth" (Matt. 12:40). But His grave was NOT literally in the heart of the earth; it was hewn out of a vertical rock wall so that a stone could close the opening.

The women waited to anoint Christ's body until after the sabbath (Luke 23:54-56). But if Christ had died on Wednesday, they could have done this deed of love on a Thursday or a Friday.

Further, Peter in Acts 2:31 quotes Psalm 16:10 to the effect that Christ's body did not "see corruption" which would likely have happened if it had remained lifeless for 72 hours.

Armstrongism twists Scripture dishonestly, as in their tract, "Rejoice in God's Sabbath!" Referring to Exodus 35:3, "Ye shall kindle no fire throughout your habitations upon the sabbath day," they make *habitations* to mean *foundries!* This is rank dishonesty—and incredible.

Of course, Armstrongites do not all live in warm Palestine, and they like hot meals on Saturdays, and they expect other people to work on Saturdays for them. So—they change habitations to foundries.

And then they suggest that we ask one of their "qualified" agents from Ambassador College to help us find God and the "true" church. Jesus said of such, "Let them alone; they are blind leaders of the blind. And if the blind lead the blind, both shall fall into the ditch" (Matt. 15:14).

But with so *many* of their "ditches," we must post more warning signs. One of their biggest ditches involves Great Britain and the United States. For Armstrongism has borrowed the old fallacy of British-Israelism, without giving credit to previous fantasy-weavers, and have made it a large part of their church. Much of this is more humor than history, as we shall see.

11

THE UNITED STATES AND
BRITISH COMMONWEALTH
IN PROPHECY

HERE WE SHALL cite as briefly as possible some of the more glaring deceptions, historical errors, and bad guesses in the book with the above title (USBCP), written by Herbert W. Armstrong (HWA), in 1967.

Mr. HWA did not invent this Anglo-Israel heresy. "The fundamentals of Anglo-Israelism were first propounded about 1790 by a harmless madman named Richard Brothers . . ." (R. L. Ray in *Apostles of Discord*, 92. Beacon press, 1953). Poor deluded Mr. Brothers died in an insane asylum.

"Incredible but true!" and "Incredible facts!" Such are HWA's favorite gambits and gimmicks which are apparently effective in disarming careless readers. Incredible—yes. Facts—no.

1. (page 3) HWA lists the great world powers of our time, but he fails to include China and Japan. (I have taught secular and church history 19 years, on college and graduate levels. But no expertise is needed to detect HWA's numerous historical blunders.)

2. (4) HWA's "Master Key" is his alleged identity of Americans, British and Germans in Biblical prophecies. This "identity" is *his* strongest proof of the authority of the Bible. But not one verse supports HWA here; his "proofs" vanish with careful reading. And since his "Master Key" is wrong, how can his work be trusted?

3. (6) HWA asserts, without support, that most Old Testa-

ment (OT) prophecies were not given to ancient Israel, but for "our people" at the present time. But "Israel" is mentioned about 2400 times in the OT; yet this one HWA proposes to cancel most prophecies of Israel on his own authority. He refers often to "The Ten Lost Tribes" but no such phrase is in the Bible. Yet he says, "Today we know," meaning that none except HWA and his group know the meanings of Biblical prophecies!

4. (8) HWA misreads history when he says that Britain did not become a great world power until the 19th century. The reign of Queen Elizabeth I (1558-1603) marked England then as truly a great world power.

5. (19) HWA's map has the city of Ur nearly straight north of Palestine, whereas it should be mostly east, and a bit south! With such ignorance of geography and history, how can we trust him in anything?

The 1972 issue of USBCP omits this absurd map, and has a few other minor "corrections." But such revisions destroy Armstrong's claim of monopoly on knowing the Bible. Like those who "prophesied" the end of the world in 1844—and then "adjusted" their predictions—even so do the Armstrongs. Their Master Key to "90 per cent of all prophecy" (HWA says) DOES NOT FIT!

6. (21) On Genesis 17:7—"And I will establish my covenant between me and thee and thy seed after thee in their generations," HWA says that "seed" is plural, but Galatians 3:16 corrects him. "He saith not, And to seeds, as of many; but as of one, And to thy seed, which is Christ."

7. (36) Quoting "the birthright was Joseph's" (1 Chron. 5:2), HWA says that this is the pivot and key to understanding ALL prophecy! But HWA's "key" is made of wax, and he molds it to suit his own prejudices. It is too much like Mrs. Eddy's Key that locks the Scriptures.

8. (52) The descendants of Ephraim and Manasseh will be numbered by the billions! Isn't this another of HWA's exaggerations?

9. (53) HWA identifies Ephraim with the British Commonwealth nations and Manasseh with the United States. Ephraim and Manasseh, says HWA, received the name "Israel" as their right; "they are not Jews." Since HWA emphasizes this repeatedly, we must show that the names "Jews" and "Israelites"

are often interchangeable. In the NT alone, "Jew" is found 193
times; "Israel" or "Israelites" 78 times. HWA insists that the NT
people were Jews only, and not of Israel. He fixes rigid prophecies on this idea.

But the NT contradicts HWA. Jesus said, "I am not sent but
unto the lost sheep of the house of Israel" (Matt. 15:24). In
John 1:47 Jesus said of Nathanael, "Behold an Israelite indeed."
John 3:1, 10—"Nicodemus, a ruler of the Jews . . . Art thou a
teacher of Israel . . .?" Acts 2:47—"For of a truth against thy
holy child Jesus . . . the people of Israel were gathered together."
Acts 2:22—"Ye men of Israel." Acts 4:8—"Ye rulers of the people,
and elders of Israel." "Twelve tribes" in Acts 26:1, James 1:1.
"Are they Israelites? so am I," said Paul, a Jew (2 Cor. 11:22;
Phil. 3:5).

Israelites and Jews are combined (Isa. 10:20-23; 11:12; 14:1;
Jer. 3:18; 5:33, 34; Hosea 1:11; Dan. 9:1-18; Ezra 2:70; 6:17, 21,
etc.).

10. (60) Because Jacob said of Joseph that he would be "a
fruitful bough by a wall, whose branches run over the wall,"
HWA says Joseph would be a colonizing people. What a strange
basis for history or prophecy! Mr. HWA goes far out on a limb
here, even to the United States.

11. (80) HWA labors again at great length to show that
Israel's ten tribes are always distinct from the Jews, and vice
versa. On the contrary, see our number 9 above, plus Matthew
4:13, 14; 10:5, 6; Luke 2:36; Acts 4:36; Philippians 3:5. Northern
and southern tribes moved and mixed during the centuries since
Joshua (1 Chron. 15:9).

12. (86) HWA says the descendants of Ephraim and Manasseh, hundreds of millions, will return to Palestine (p. 113, 114).
Then Israel will need to conquer much more land in order to
make room for so many.

13. (67) HWA says the prophecy in 2 Samuel 7:13 does not
mean that Christ will have the throne of Jacob forever. Correction: Luke 1:32, 33.

14. (87, 88) The Samaritans, says HWA, were not all a mix-
ture with the people of Israel. But see 2 Chronicles 30:18; 34:6;
Ezra 4:3 and about 20 references to Israelites in the book of
Nehemiah, for example.

15. (89) The returned exiles and Ezra who rebuilt the temple,

after 70 years of captivity, were from Judah only, says HWA. But Nehemiah returned *after* Ezra, and Nehemiah mentioned *Israel* 20 times. (See this author's book *Nehemiah the Executive*, published in 1954. Revised edition 1973, *Nehemiah for Us Now*).

16. (89) HWA says all Israelites were completely removed to Assyria (2 Kings 17:23), but better historians say many remained. How else could the Samaritans have a religion so similar to Judaism?

17. (97) On many pages, HWA says immodestly that no one except himself has known the real meaning of end-time prophecies. He ignores the vast number of dedicated, intelligent, spirit-filled scholars with thorough knowledge of Bible languages —which HWA lacks—and who are more credible. And HWA is dogmatic! He is so very sure of himself. In his *Plain Truth*, Sept. 1971, page 2, he wrote "The General (Carlos P. Romulo of Manila) had been looking forward to meeting me for some time."

18. (103) HWA asserts that after Jeremiah was taken to Egypt (he was old then), he returned to Judah and then—of all places —went to *Ireland!* But better historians say he was stoned to death in Egypt. More, he was a Benjamite, and therefore could not be one of HWA's exclusivist "Israelites."

On July 26, 1971, I wrote to Armstrong's headquarters: What proof or documentation do you have for saying that Jeremiah went to Ireland? The reply came August 27, 1971: "You can find the history in O'Flaherty's *Ogygia*." But Dr. McKiernon of the Irish-American Center at St. Thomas College in St. Paul, Minnesota (he is probably "the best expert on early Irish history in the entire midwest"), wrote about Jeremiah in Ireland: "This is not asserted by a single scholar on early Irish history anywhere; absolutely no one in Irish history puts his name to it."

O'Flaherty's *Ogygia* has no historical value at all; it is a collection of folk lore; it is early lore and traditions. There is absolutely no shred of evidence for it and no reputable person in Irish history believes it. But Armstrongism builds its system on such folk lore!

19. (103) Apart from ANY proof, HWA arbitrarily makes Isaiah 37:31, 32 and 2 Kings 19:30, 31 refer to Jeremiah.

20. (105) HWA says that "history" tells of Zarah's descendants becoming wanderers, going northward among Scythian nations,

and their posterity going later to Ireland during King David's reign. Note that HWA fails to cite *which history*. It looks like sheer fabrication, and very doubtful.

HWA makes much of "overturn, overturn, overturn" (Ezek. 21:27), saying it means that Jeremiah would set up a dynasty in Ireland, then it was to be "overturned" to Scotland, and again to England (109)! But another version of Ezekiel 21:27 has it, "A ruin, ruin, ruin will I make it; there shall not be even a trace of it until he comes whose right it is; and to him will I give it." This undermines Armstrong. And who but Christ has a right to the throne? as Scofield's note wisely suggests.

A pleasing contrast to HWA's fictional migrations of Jeremiah and Israel is Thor Heyerdahl's *Kon-Tiki* and *Ra* expeditions, both in recent years. *Kon-tiki* proved that ancient South American Indians could have sailed westward to Polynesia where relics and legends have amazing likenesses to those of ancient Peru.

Likewise, Central and South America have 60 items of culture similar to ancient Mesopotamia and Egypt. In comparison, does HWA have ANY similar evidence of Israelites migrating to the British Isles? With NO traces of Hebrew words or customs, such as circumcision and sabbaths in Britain, what bases does HWA have except his own fictional imagination? This is a false foundation for theology.

21. (107) HWA makes Ezekiel 12:9 refer to "ten-tribed Israel" but 12:10 says the reference is to the "prince in Jerusalem." And Ezekiel refers to Judah 15 times, e.g., "the elders of Judah sat before me" (8:1). This was during the exile, when HWA says no Israelites were in Palestine, but 12:10 says the "house of Israel" was there!

"Heads I win; tails you lose" is HWA's method of "explaining" the Bible.

One wonders if HWA and/or his writers ever studied Hermeneutics.

22. (107ff) HWA's fanciful and arbitrary "interpretation" of Ezekiel 17:22-24 is a glaring example of his bad exegesis. The "tender twig" is a daughter of Zedekiah and a "tree" is a nation! So HWA, like Alice in Wonderland, can make any word mean anything he wants it to mean. Here he tries to perpetuate the kingly line of Zedekiah, even if he has to go to Ireland to do it, *with a mythical daughter-twig*. But the Bible contradicts him

again. "For the children of Israel shall abide many days *without a king,* and without a prince . . ." (Hosea 3:4). A "twig" is wobbly support for HWA.

23. (109) Entirely without ANY authority, support or documentation, HWA rashly says "Israel" had lived independently in Ireland 400 years, since the time of King David, that Israel had a kingly line connected with Zedekiah's daughter, and that Irish Israelites were never captured by the Assyrians! But he MUST have Israel in the British Isles, somehow.

I once watched a little boy working at his arithmetic problems. He needed an 8 from somewhere to make his answer come out right. So—he simply added an 8. "Where did you get that 8?" his brother asked him. "Never mind where I got it. I needed it, and now my answer is right." We shall refer to HWA's similar scheme in several later sections.

24. (111, 112) Mr. Armstrong "knows" the ten tribes of Israel exist now as a nation, and a group of nations, considered as Gentiles. But he conveniently omits support of his unhistorical assumptions. If this is history, then comic sections in newspapers are science.

Three very learned professors in Hebrew languages and history, Dr. Maurice Price, Dr. Ovid Sellers, and Dr. E. Leslie Carlson, wrote—"But there is no people or nation or tongue today that can be identified as the 'ten lost tribes.' " (*The Monuments and the Old Testament,* 262, 263). From Dean R. G. Grant in *The Plain Truth about the Armstrong Cult.*

25. (112) HWA mistakenly says that Jeremiah was commissioned to do the "planting" of the Israelites' throne in Ireland. But Jeremiah was a prophet, not a king-maker, as Jeremiah 1:10 declares.

26. (113) HWA headlines, "Lost ISRAEL Located!" HWA's detective work led him to Hosea 12:1, "Ephraim feedeth on wind, and followeth after the east wind; he daily increaseth lies and desolation." (HWA omits this last clause!) But look at HWA's logic: since an east wind blows westward, *therefore,* Ephraim (the ten tribes) went westward from Assyria! So, Armstrong's history is actually *based on wind.*

27. (113) But HWA needs more; he wants Ephraim on an island. Easy. Find a convenient 8; look in a concordance; find the word wanted. HWA found it in Psalm 89:25, "I will set his

hand also in the sea, and his right hand in the rivers." Now he is at sea, but very dishonestly he changes "hand" to "sceptre." He knows full well that few will check up on him. But the Hebrew word for "hand" in Psalm 89:25 is *yad*, whereas "sceptre" is *shebat* or *sharebit*. How incredible can he get?

Since HWA cannot be trusted on one hand, why trust him with another?

28. (113) Again HWA needs a convenient word (another 8); this time he needs "north." Among the 150 places in the OT where it is found, he chose Jeremiah 3:7–12, a passage very remote from his "east wind" of Hosea 12:1. And Judah is mentioned four times in this passage, although HWA wants *Israel* in Ireland, not Judah!

29. (114) HWA takes the King James Version of "coasts" to mean shore lines, whereas any good Bible student knows the word means "borders" even apart from shores. But HWA wants Israel in Britain, regardless.

30. (114) "Sinim" is mentioned in Isaiah 49:12. HWA tries to make this mean British Australia, asking help here of the Catholic Vulgate. But the new Catholic Bible has Sinim to be Syene, as does the rsv. Syene is at the first cataract of the Nile, near where the Asswan Dam is located.

31. (115) HWA says the Hebrews never pronounced their "h," but they did. It is their fifth letter of the alphabet. Dr. Kyle M. Yates' Hebrew grammar says it is like "h" in "hat" And most Englishmen would be vexed by HWA's saying they do not pronounce "h."

32. Copying previous cultists, HWA tries to make the Hebrew *berith* (covenant) and *ish* (man) to mean "men of the covenant." This is trickery with words, to make *berith* and *ish* to mean British. For "British" is from ancient Latin, *britto;* and *ish* is simply a common English suffix used to form adjectives, such as "childish" and "foolish."

Mr. Armstrong mistakes homonyms for synonyms—a poor base for theology!

33. (116) Another HWA scrabble game: "Saxons" are "Isaac's sons!" But "Saxon" is from the Latin, *Saxo;* plural, *Saxones.* The Hebrew "Isaac" means laughter (Gen. 17:17; 18:12–15; 21:6— laughter is mentioned seven times). If the reader's pent-up laughter needs to explode here, let it. Imagine HWA discover-

ing more theology in Jer USA lem? And Anderson in Galatians
4:30! Some wag found Seers, Roebuck Company in Isaiah 29:10;
Deuteronomy 14:5; Genesis 35:11! Seriously, the Semitic-Hebrew
has nothing in common with Anglo-Saxon, as any history of the
English language will reveal.

34. (116–118) HWA makes the tribe of Dan to be prolific
and ubiquitous. Omitting the vowel, any place with DN must
mean that "Dan was there." So HWA identifies DeNmark,
DuNdee, DoN, DaNau, DaNube, DNieper, LonDon, DiNgle,
etc. These are HWA's own proofs. (DuNsmore means "more
Dans!") What could he do with Manasseh? MaiNe, MaNitoba,
MaNila, MaNagua, MaNassas!

35. (116) HWA asserts that the German Saxons are quite
different from those who migrated to England. Proof? None.

36. (117) HWA says the Danites, at the time Assyria captured
Israel, sailed westward and then to Ireland, leaving many names
with "DN." He refers to Irish "annals" but does not name them
as folk lore.

37. (118) HWA refers to unnamed old annals, legends, and
histories of Ireland which are alleged to tell of Jeremiah's
"planting" and the present location of the ten lost tribes. HWA
can "easily" sort out the legend from real history, he says. One
wonders.

38. (118) Before 700 bc, says HWA, some Danites arrived in
Ireland. Then, "later" (?), during David's reign the descendants
of Zarah came to Ireland from the Near East. But King David
reigned from 1011 to 971 bc, which is certainly not later than
700 bc.

39. (118) HWA refers to "Jeremiah's transplanting" in 569 bc,
but he gives no authority for this date, or of his bringing Jeremiah
to Ireland. Without proof, he names "Tea-Tephi" as a daughter
of Zedekiah.

40. (121) Now comes the famous "Stone of Scone." HWA
says Jeremiah brought it with him to Ireland where it was called
"lia-fail." This was the stone Jacob used for his pillow (Gen.
28:11, 18), an *uncut* stone. But the Stone of Scone is a quarried
(cut) stone, and such must not be used as an altar (Exo. 20:25;
Gen. 28:18). Professor A. C. Ramsey, London University geolo-
gist, tested this Stone of Scone chemically and microscopically
and called it "calcareous sandstone of Scottish origin."

41. (122) HWA makes the incredible statement that this "King Herremon's" dynasty has continued unbroken to the present reign of Queen Elizabeth II! But English history records several dynasties as the Tudor, Plantagenet, Lancaster, Stuart, Hanover, and now Windsor.

And if HWA's "Israelite" throne is now in London, what need is there for a "restoration," or for the second coming of Chirst to bring in HWA's kind of kingdom?

42. (123) HWA says that Christ will sit on that throne, with its Stone of Scone. And the British group of nations was the ONLY company of nations in history! What about the once vast Roman Empire? And the USSR? And he claims again that the United States is Manasseh.

43. (126) Our United States began with 13 colonies; Manasseh was the 13th tribe; therefore, "we are Manasseh." Such proof, HWA says, is "overwhelming." The USA has been a melting pot for dozens of nationalities for centuries, with constant intermarriages—yet we are Manasseh!

44. (128) Historian HWA says he has "ample evidence" that eight of the ten lost tribes of Israel settled in Holland, Belgium, Denmark, northern France, Luxembourg, Switzerland, Sweden, Norway, and Iceland. But does he cite ANY evidence? None.

45. Incidentally, Jacob blessed Ephraim above Manasseh (Gen. 48:14-20) but now HWA's Manasseh-USA is greater than his Ephraim-England.

46. (130) Great Britain has had Australia since 1770, but HWA says it was not until after 1800. A minor matter, perhaps.

47. (134) HWA implies, from Leviticus 26, that God blessed the United States and Great Britain from 1800 on, but these two nations have always honored Sundays as opposed to the Sabbaths of Leviticus 26:2.

48. (136) HWA quotes the terrible punishments for not obeying "all these commandments" including the Sabbaths of the OT, yet the US and GB never have been punished as HWA says. Also, we were blessed before 1800.

49. (137) HWA says Israel's population in Moses' time was two or three millions, but in his "Which Day is the Christian Sabbath" he said it was three or four millions.

50. (143) HWA says Judah seceded from the rest of Israel. He is wrong; it was Israel, or the ten northern tribes, that

seceded from Judah (1 Kings 12:1–33). And again HWA says these ten tribes were never called Jews. To see his mistake, consult any good concordance.

51. (143) HWA refers to "ample evidence" that Jeroboam I observed the first day of the week instead of the sabbath. But he fails to cite one iota of such "evidence." It must be that he could find none. Who can?

52. (144ff) HWA uses the "day for a year" principle to "prove" that Israel was to be punished 2520 years, beginning with 720 BC. This adds up to 1800 AD, the date he wanted. (See # 23 above.) But HWA's Hebrew years have only 360 days each; he is short 5¼ days in each of 2520 years; this means he is short 13,230 days, or about 36¼ years. Back up to 1774!

53. (147) HWA's reference to punishing Israel seven times more for their sins is the basis of his cunning arithmetic. "Times" has to mean years—in order to accommodate HWA. But the "times" are repeated in Leviticus 26:21, 24, 28 so that HWA must add 2520 years for each of these verses. This would postpone his prophecy (?) until the year 9360 AD! And yet HWA says this is the most important prophecy in the Bible!

54. (148) The punishment described in Leviticus 26 for disobeying the commandments, such as the OT sabbaths, have NOT characterized the US or Great Britain. They may have occurred in Palestine, but not here.

55. (149) HWA cites wrong references; he wonders why, after Acts 15:29 we never after read of the 12 apostles. Except for Peter going to Babylon, HWA has the Twelve all gone to lost Israel. But the Twelve are mentioned about 20 times after his erroneous Acts 15:29.

56. (149) Jesus told His disciples to go "to the lost sheep of the house of Israel" (Matt. 10:5, 6). This HAS to mean those in Palestine at that time, but HWA says No. He said on page 115 (USBCP) they had gone to northwestern Europe! And HWA would have Christ sending the Twelve to Europe, a 5000-mile round trip, without supplies, and all within a few weeks!

57. (149) HWA says Jesus never urged anyone to get saved, but He did! His call to "Repent!" was a plea to get saved (Matt. 4:17; 11:28; 23:37; Luke 19:10; John 6:29, 37–51). HWA says the same about the apostles, but see Acts 2:38; 11:14; Romans 9:1–3; 10:1; 1 Thessalonians 2:16, etc.

59. (149) HWA implies that the British Isles had heard Christ's gospel in the days of the Druids, but he gives no evidence for it. None exists.

59. (149) In 1800, says HWA, the US and GB suddenly became the greatest world powers in history. But France then, under Napoleon, was stronger than England, and the US had very little power at that time.

60. (151) Again HWA writes "incredible facts." Incredible, yes; facts, no. He does write incredible history, incredible prophecy, and incredible theology. Of course he is not 100% wrong on everything, but his half-truths can be worse than lies.

61. (156) Here HWA reverses the road signs again. He says Christian ministers are actually Satan's ministers. He should look in a mirror while reading 2 Corinthians 11:14, 15. An upstart cultist calls all Christian ministers Satan's! Such incredible gall! "Woe unto them that call evil good, and good evil; who put darkness for light, and light for darkness; who put bitter for sweet, and sweet for bitter" (Isa. 5:20).

Mr. H. W. Armstrong accuses the hundreds of thousands of intelligent, Spirit-filled, fruitful, *Christian* ministers of being Satan's tools. He is like the mother watching her soldier-son marching. She said, "They are all out of step but my Jim!"

Satan is the great accuser of our brethren (Rev. 12:10). Since HWA uses his vast media for accusing us, then *he* is on the devil's side. "Things equal to the same thing are equal to each other."

Consider the vast good Christian churches are doing. They do just what Christ did—teaching, preaching, and healing. More: loving, comforting, fellowshiping, helping, nursing, warning, feeding, clothing, praying for, and saving people all over the world. Suday School teachers give years and years, freely, to their difficult work. We have built churches, hospitals, schools, orphanages, old people's homes, dispensaries, printing houses, rescue homes, rest homes—*all in Christ's Name.* "By their fruits ye shall know them." Christians have GOOD fruit.

What "fruit" does HWA have? More propaganda *against* Christ's body, His churches and Christian works. HWA *attacks* Christ's body.

62. (157) Now HWA takes off on the sabbath again. He falsified 2 Corinthians 3:6–17 which deals with the Ten Commandments. The OT sabbath is "done away, abolished" in Christ.

But in HWA's confusion he says that to observe Christ's resurrection on Sundays is a pagan custom, contrary to God's command. He is terribly wrong.

63. (158) HWA tries hard to show that only his particular followers are the people of God. But *what have they done* for Christ and the world? What *good* comes from Armstrong's propaganda? His colleges, magazines, and broadcasts are meant to *hinder* and *ruin* real Christian work.

Has Armstrongism built any hospitals? Orphanages? Retirement homes? Rescue missions? Has he pioneered any missionary work? Has he done any Bible translation work, such as the Wycliffe people? Has he had any soul-winning revivals anywhere? But his college graduates go everywhere, trying to hinder our good Christian ministries all over the world.

64. (159) HWA emphasizes Exodus 31:13 about God "sanctifying" Israel. But in our time—think of 6,000,000 Jews killed by Hitler's hirelings. And the Jews now in Israel are 70% atheistic, it is reported.

65. (159) HWA says to keep the sabbath and then your friends will set you apart. But this is far different from sanctification. One can do any number of foolish things such as being dirty, chewing tobacco, and constant bragging, and thus one will be "set apart."

As for true Christians losing popularity, we read that instead they had "favor with all the people" (Acts 2:47).

66. (160) HWA makes the OT sabbath command the *only* one that identifies true Christians today. To line up with Christ-hating Jews is thus commended. To honor OT laws, meant for Israel *only*, in place of the Christians' Lord's Day, does not seem to be Christian at all.

"By this shall all men know that ye are my disciples, if ye have love one to another" Jesus said in John 13:35. But HWA promotes *ill* will, distrust, and separation from such loving Christians. He says we are Satan's people because we keep Sundays. (Now HWA may accuse me of name-calling in these pages, because I expose him, and tell it like it is. But I follow the example of Christ (Matt. 23), of Paul (2 Tim. 3, 4), of Peter (2 Peter 2), and of Jude (8–19) in identifying Christ-denying errors and in warning true Christians against such false cultists as the Armstrongs.)

67. (161) Again HWA identifies the "real" people of God with his own brand of sabbatarians. But his media do not exhibit the nine-fold fruit of the Spirit (Gal. 5:22, 23). "By their fruits ye shall know them." And we know the fruits of Armstrongism: proselytism, legalism, formalism, separatism, egotism, criticism, and pharisaism.

68. (162) HWA tries to separate the sabbath covenant in Exodus 31 from the Ten Commandments in Exodus 20. But Exodus 31 stipulates that the sabbath is for Israel only, and 2 Corinthians 3:6–17 says that all Ten Commandments are now superseded by Christ's higher and better laws.

69. (162) HWA emphasizes the word "forever" in Exodus 31:17. This word is the Hebrew *olam,* meaning "for an age." It is so used in 1 Samuel 28:2; 1 Kings 12:7 and elsewhere. It does not always mean endless, any more than does "perpetual care" at cemeteries. Just as a will is valid only until a new one, or a codicil, is added, so the OT covenants were binding only until the NT came into effect with Christ. The Book of Hebrews makes this very clear.

70. (163) HWA consigns to "the lake of fire" those who disagree with *him.* But the OT sabbath was binding on Israel only until the NT became effective. And the British and Americans are NOT Israelites. HWA mistakenly refers us to Galatians 3:28, 29 which combines Jews and Greeks, male and female, into one body or church. When we Gentiles become Christians we have faith like Abraham's and thus are "heirs according to the promise." We can no more become Israelites than they can become Gentiles.

71. (164) HWA refers again to the "lost ten tribes" but this phrase contradicts James 1:1 and 1 Peter 1:1. They knew the ten tribes were not lost; so did Josephus later *(Antiquities* ix, 5, 1–2). Paul referred to Jews 25 times, meaning ALL Israelites, for he never made any distinction between Jews and Israelites. Paul himself was a Jew (Acts 21:39; 22:3); he was also an Israelite (2 Cor. 11:22; Phil. 3:5).

72. (165) Again HWA says that Jeroboam changed the sabbath to the first day of the week. But not one verse says so. (Sorry, some of our repetitions *are* needed. The Bible has a great deal of repetition.) 2 Kings 4:23 indicates that Israel kept sabbaths many years after Jeroboam. HWA says Sunday is the

pagan day of the sun! What about Saturnday? That IS a pagan name. We Christians do not worship the sun. We do know it outshines Saturn. And the sun typifies God (Psalm 84:11).

73. (166) HWA is sure the Assyrians, before 604 BC, migrated to Germany, and are now the German people. Documentation? None.

74. (166) The tribe of Reuben settled in France! HWA says so.

75. (168) HWA seems to blame God for the King James translation of 1 John 3:4, insisting it covers sabbath laws. But the verse really says, "sin is lawlessness *(anomia)*" and since it was written late in the first century, it *has to* mean NT laws, not OT Jewish laws.

76. (169) HWA repeats his Israel-to-Europe trek, over and over. Hitler said, "repeat a lie often enough and people will believe it." Not all.

77. (171) We deny that Ezekiel says Israel kept Sundays, but we do admit that they polluted their sabbaths (Ezek. 20:21).

78. (171) HWA, in 1967, prophesied awful things in seven to ten years, but on page vii of this 1967 book he said *five* years. Confusion.

79. (172) HWA lists himself with Noah, Elijah, and John the Baptist!

80. (175) HWA cites Robert Fulton's steamboat in 1803 (first on Hudson River in 1807), the railroads, and some "gates" as fulfillment of prophecy. Also, the Louisiana Purchase of 1803 is in *his* prophecy.

One traveler bragged to another, "I saw an old city dug up and they found lots of old wires, proving they knew all about telephones and telegraphs." Retort: "I saw an old city dug up and no wires were found; this proves that they knew all about wireless telegraphy!"

81. (175ff) Economic facts cited by HWA are gratifying but pointless. Both the US and GB began losing much economic superiority about the time HWA began broadcasting. Cause and effect not claimed.

82. (180) HWA asks if US and GB are not actual inheritors of the "Birthright" blessings which were to be bestowed, beginning in 1803 AD, then who else can be? But where is 1803 in

the Bible? or 1800? or the US? or GB? But HWA says 1803 is "precisely" the prophesied time! Incredible.

83. (184) "Other prophecies," says HWA, reveal that probably by 1971 we will have drouth, famine, and disease taking millions of lives. But the earth, in every generation, has had drouths, famines and diseases. And to save his jumbled comments on "seven times" (Lev. 26:18), HWA insists that the wording of Leviticus 26:21 is entirely different from v. 18. He would be in more trouble if he heeded vs. 24 and 28 which also have "seven times."

84. (185) How does HWA explain God allowing the US and GB so much prestige and wealth when we have never kept his OT sabbaths? And why does he seem to gloat over the awful doom he predicts for the US and GB?

85. (193) HWA is badly confused in comparing the US and GB to the lion in Micah 5:8 that goes among "flocks of sheep" and "treadeth down, and teareth in pieces." So HWA makes the carnivorous, destructive lion the symbol of English-speaking nations preserving the world's peace! Any animal that "treadeth down and teareth in pieces" is hardly a peacemaker.

86. (195) HWA is dogmatic in saying the English-speaking people fulfill "precisely" the prophecy in Hosea 5:7–15. He could as easily put a square peg into a round hole and make it fit precisely. The US and GB have done more good to the world, perhaps, than all other nations combined, yet HWA focuses his wrath upon them, especially on England. Is it because the English refused him permission for his radio propaganda there?

87. (198) HWA points again his most intense punishment upon Britain and America. Is it because we are too slow in accepting his OT sabbath? HWA calls the "virgin daughter of Babylon" in Isaiah 47:1 a church. It seems that he needed another "8" to make his answer come out right.

88. (199) HWA is positive that contemporary Germans are actually descendants of Assyrians. Thus, any prophecy concerning Assyria must, as of now, conveniently mean modern Germany. HWA says so. And the ancient Babylonians, or Chaldeans, settled in Italy, according to HWA.

89. (206) HWA is able to see in Hosea's prophecy the precise, concise, and specific *attitude* of Britain-America right *now*. In

Hosea 1:6–11 he sees the picture of God's entire dealing with Israel, meaning US and GB. The fact is, neither nation is ever mentioned or described in the Bible.

90. (208) HWA is positive that Hosea 4:16 speaks of modern Britain. Since England refused him a radio license, he began broadcasting from some "pirate" ships, thus forcing his messages upon England which has enough troubles without HWA. And the US has increasing lawlessness partly because cultists like Jehovah's Witnesses and Armstrongites have done their utmost to destroy the good influence of our pastors and churches. For these pastors and churches have been the greatest barrier to crime. Thus when HWA attacks us *he is on the side of lawlessness.* Is he not then guilty of the sin mentioned in 1 John 3:4?

91 (211) HWA loves to pick out verses of future doom and apply them to all groups but his own. The more obscure and difficult those verses are, the better for his purposes; he knows few will bother to check up on him. And such allusions emphasize his superior (!) wisdom (210). HWA molds his prophecies, like soft clay, to fit the mold he wants. If his Biblical mold is difficult he adjusts it; thus Ephraim becomes England.

"What is at first a bare possibility is turned into a surmise; a surmise soon becomes a likelihood; the likelihood becomes an extreme probability and ends by becoming a dogmatic certainty!!" (W. C. Irvine, *Ibid.*, 25.)

92. (211) To safeguard all true Armstrongites, HWA takes them to an unnamed place of safety. But they must remain true *to him* for life, or else! To remain true they must send in their tithes, and then some.

93. One wonders how the British people (Ephraim) suddenly were transformed into Manasseh as soon as they landed in America!

If this point, and many others in HWA, strikes the reader as comical, perhaps the next chapter will not be needed. However, some Armstrongites may feel a tension. For all of us who get "up tight" on occasion, a good laugh brings relief. Even our biggest officials in Washington, D. C., laugh at themselves most heartily when the annual Gridiron Club lampoons them. This author—who is not a pope—can laugh at himself as well.

"A merry heart doeth good like medicine" (Prov. 17:22).

Since writing this chapter, I secured and read THE MARSON REPORT CONCERNING H. W. ARMSTRONG. This 175-page book exposes HWA's UNITED STATES AND BRITISH COMMONWEALTH IN PROPHECY. Mr. Marson was for ten years a trusted member and leader in Armstrongism. Upon checking his Bible, he found many serious errors, dangerous ones, in HWA; he lists them in this book. Mr. Marson was also amused at many of HWA's naive, fantastic, and grotesque blunders.

12

A DIFFERENT PERSPECTIVE

HERE WE GIVE some ludicrous examples of faulty reasoning, non sequitors, lack of logic, sophistry, flimsy bases for erroneous conclusions, wrong uses of synonyms for homonyms. Mr. Armstrong and other cultists use such to support their impossible assertions. A bit of humor may give us a wholesome perspective. No personal offence is intended.

"Many doubts are so absurd that the only way to combat them is by gentle ridicule" (C. H. Spurgeon).

          ❖ ❖ ❖

Many years ago, in an examination for ordination, a man was asked to tell the story of the Prodigal Son.

"Well, suh, onct upon a time a man went down from Jerusalem to Jericho, and fell among thieves. And de thorns grew up and choked dat man; and he went on and he didn't have no money. And he met de Queen of Sheba, and behold, she gave dat man a thousand talents of gold and a hundred changes of raiment. (No irreverence or racism is intended here.)

"And he got in a chariot straightway and drove furiously, and as he was speeding along under a big sycamore tree his har got caught in a limb and left him hangin' dere. And he hung dere many days and many nights, and de ravens brought him food to eat and water to drink.

"And one night while he was hangin' dere asleep, his wife Delilah came along and cut off his hair, and de poah man

92

dropped and fell on stony ground. So de man went out into de highways an' came to Jerusalem, and when he got dere he seen Queen Jezebel sittin' high up in a window, and when he saw her he said aloud, 'Trow her down.' And dey trew her down.

"And he cried again, 'Trow her down some moah'; and dey trew her down some moah. And dey trew her down seventy times seven, and seventy of de fragments was picked up twelve baskets. Now whose wife you all think she be in de resurrection?"

* * *

Some words sound alike. Saxons is like Isaac's sons. Deaf people have trouble here, sometimes amusingly so to everyone but themselves.

A certain family had a dog named Paddy, of whom they were very fond. He was the special pet of the young son. Too bad, but the dog ran in front of a car. Freddie was at school, and the mother tried to break the news gently, told of Paddy's death. To her surprise, Freddie took it calmly. Later the boy came sobbing into the house. "Paddy's dead," he wailed. "Yes," said mama, "I told you before, but you took no notice." "Yes, but I thought you said Daddy."

* * *

Two young women were concerned, in a book store, about selecting something in fiction. "This one looks gloomy, '*The Last Days of Pompeii*' said one. "What did he die of?" "I'm not sure," ventured the other, "but I think it was some kind of eruption."

* * *

"No new thing under the sun," said Solomon. Not even fads in theology.

An old widower went back to his boyhood home and married his childhood sweetheart. Taking her back to his home he introduced her to his children as their "new mama." Then his small son drew his father's head down and whispered into his ear, "Pop, you're sold! She's not new; she's old!"

* * *

In a recent civil service examination for men to join the Los Angeles Police force, the following were some answers given. Q: What would you do in case of a race riot? A: Get the number of both cars. Q: What is sabotage? A: Breaking the laws of the

sabbath. Q: What are rabies and what would you do for them?
A: Rabies are Jewish priests and I would not do anything for
them.

* * *

"How much are two times two?" a facetious student in logic
asked his young sister. "Four," she responded confidently.

"No, but you must use deductive reasoning," said big brother.
"We all know that one times one is one; therefore, two times
two must be two." Sister kept silent. "Let's try again," said he.
"Two times two means two two's. Right? Now look at your
calendar—any calendar. See that number between 21 and 23?
Doesn't that mean that two times two are 22? That is inductive
reasoning." Sister said, "I'll stay with four."

We plan to stay with four in this book, regardless of cultist
logic.

* * *

From his plane, Doc Hall saw a bear cub walking in circles.
Its head was stuck tightly in an empty can. With a rescue party,
they tranquilized the bear, snipped the can off its head, and
then took off. When last seen, the bear was walking in a straight
line.

How much will it take to remove the can of legalism, or the
veil, from Armstrong's people (2 Cor. 3:15–18)?

13

BEWARE OF FOLLOWING
STRANGERS!

JESUS SAID, "AND a stranger will they not follow, but will flee from him; for they know not the voice of strangers" (John 10:5). "They" in this verse means those of us who love and obey Christ as our Savior and Lord, with no dictator-cultist between Him and us.

Is the Armstrong cult one of these strangers? Let us see—

1. Herbert W. Armstrong (HWA) and his henchmen are constantly fighting our churches, most of which are no worse or better than the first New Testament church. We KNOW that Christ loves our churches. "Christ loved the church and gave himself for it" (Eph. 5:25). *HWA does just the opposite*. He fights us. What Christ tries to build up (Matt. 16:18) HWA tries to destroy. This is enough to identify Armstrongism as a false cult.

Rev. E. B. Rockstad, one who has had much experience in dealing with demon-possessed people, wrote me 8-23-71, "It certainly would seem that the 'seducing spirits and doctrines of devils' (1 Tim. 4:1) are involved in the teachings of Armstrong."

And Salem Kirban has a 54-page book entitled, *Doctrines of Devils No. 1, Armstrong's Church of God*. The *Dr. Jekyll and Mr. Hyde* story is much like the record of Armstrongism.

2. HWA boasts that he is THE prophet, as of "the first Sunday in January, 1934," at ten o'clock in the morning. And he says that Christ had foretold this epochal event! It was the beginning

95

of the fulfillment of 90% of all Bible prophecies. Who says so? HWA says so. HE is the self-appointed, self-announced, self-authorized, and self-advertised prophet, the first real gospel preacher since 70 A.D. HWA says so. But the Lord has some stern, pointed words about such boastful people. Notice—

a. "Then the Lord said unto me, The prophets prophesy lies in my name. *I sent them not,* neither have I commanded them, neither spoke unto them; they prophesy unto you a false vision and divination, and a thing of nought, and the deceit of their heart" (Jer. 14:14).

b. *I have not sent* these prophets, yet they ran; I have not spoken to them, yet they prophesied" (Jer. 23:21).

c. "For *I have not sent them,* saith the Lord, yet they prophesy a lie in my name, that I might drive you out, and that ye might perish, yea, ye and the prophets that prophesy unto you" (Jer. 27:15).

d. "For they prophesy falsely unto you in my name; *I have not sent them,* saith the Lord" (Jer. 29:9).

3. HWA preaches a constant message of distrust, ill will, and bitterness toward all, good and bad, in all churches but his own. He says those who worship on Sundays are Satan's people, and even the Seventh Day Adventists come under his condemnation for not keeping the OT feasts. Items—

a. "This religious Babylon" is a phrase he uses against our churches. How evil, how hateful, how malicious it is, thus to slander Christians in our churches who are Spirit-filled, devout, honest, courteous, Bible-believing, and intelligent Bible readers. Satan leads HWA to slander us.

b. "Clever counterfeit" is another phrase HWA uses to attack millions of REAL Christians all over the world. The Lord hates such bitterness. The Lord hates anyone "that soweth discord among the brethren" (Prov. 6:19).

c. HWA accuses all churches but his own of deceiving the world. Recall that Christ's deadly foes called HIM a deceiver (Matt. 27:63). The Holy Spirit said "many deceivers are entered into the world" (2 John 7).

d. HWA lumps Christians into his phrase, "quarreling denominations" but it is he who quarrels, attacks, accuses, and vilifies Christians. Most denominations do not quarrel at all; they talk friendly mergers instead; they want to unite. But HWA keeps on assailing, stabbing, insulting, and injuring every group but his own. Such attacks are (were) typical of most of the cults listed in our chapter three.

e. "False ministers" is another spiteful epithet used against all pastors, good or bad, but his own. Thus he seeks to divide Christians, but God told us to "mark them which cause divisions and offenses contrary to the doctrine which ye have learned, and avoid them" (Rom. 16:17).

f. "Insipid and inane" are some of the discourteous words he uses about our churches. A real Christian would not be that insulting. But HWA dares to do what the holy angel Michael dared not do, even against the very worst enemy, the devil. Michael dared "not bring a railing accusation, but said, The Lord rebuke thee" (Jude 9). But HWA carries on a constant railing accusation *against the Lord's best people.*

g. HWA stigmatizes our churches of hypocrisy and vicious fighting, but *he is the fighter.* And he boasts of worldwide coverage.

h. HWA and his writers condemn real Christians as "praying to gods" with reference to our service men. Who needs prayers more than soldiers?

i. HWA implies that our Judeo-Christian society is responsible for the world being near nuclear annihilation. So he blames Christians and Jews more than the Hitlers, Tojos, Mao Tse Tungs, and other atheists.

j. Why does HWA and his ilk hate us so much? Is it because we "stand fast in the liberty wherewith Christ has made us free?" "He that troubleth you shall bear his judgment, whosoever he be." "I would they were even cut off who trouble you." "For all the law is fulfilled in one word, even in this: Thou shalt love thy neighbor as thyself."

k. HWA blames God for his three business failures (*A True History,* 26). Could these failures have caused HWA's lifelong bitterness? In all the Bible, did God ever call a *single* failure into His service? Jeremiah's many references to self-appointed prophets seem to fit HWA as well as Joe Smith, Mrs. White, Mrs. Besant, Father Divine, and many others.

IF the devil had wanted someone specially trained to attack, harass, and hamper good Christian churches, how could he have done better than to employ a cunning advertising man with many tricks of psychology? His first and easiest victims would be those who had some resentment toward a church, or a pastor, or a parent, or a spouse. With shrewd insinuations and subtle suggestions, such resentment would grow and expand until the victim would believe everything HWA wrote, and deny everything a loving and devout Christian might say.

"By this shall all men *know* that ye are my disciples, if ye have love one to another" Christ said in John 13:35.

While love is conspicuously missing in much of HWA's colorful propaganda, animosity and ill will are prominent. "If a man says, I love God, and hateth his brother, he is a liar" (1 John 4:20). Too bad.

Communists hate us with deadly venom; so-called Jehovah's Witnesses call us "Satan's organization"; Mormons proselyte us unceasingly; and now we also have Armstrongites worming their way into our homes via radio and "free" literature, followed by highly trained propagandists.

Every fisherman offers a free worm to the fish he wants to hook! So HWA's literature repeats endlessly that their material is free—until the prospect is hooked. Then the financial pressure really begins.

Every kidnapper offers a free ride to the victim he plans to exploit!

Every racketeer and blackmailer offers "protection" to those who pay.

So, beware of strangers. Christ warns us, *now*. Flee from them.

But how does one identify slippery strangers? We shall soon learn.

14

ARMSTRONG'S INCREDIBLE "CHURCH"

ONE OF ARMSTRONG's stable of writers is Herman L. Hoeh (HLH) who has done a "True History of the True Church." His "home work" was not good.

He began by smearing all major denominations; this served *his* purpose in preparing a dark background for his own "true" church. For name-calling, Armstrong's writers are experts. All churches but theirs are "religious babylon." Such a vicious charge is not correct, careful, courteous or Christian. It violates the truth.

HLH wants his readers to believe that all pastors and missionaries have been deceiving the people. And of course only Armstrongism is 100% correct, in his opinion.

But Armstrong's "church" began only in 1934. And he says, without modesty or hesitancy, that the true gospel had not existed since 70 A.D. This leaves a big blank space of 1,864 years.

Strange—that millions of Bible readers never saw what HLH now sees. Or, if they saw it, they rejected it. We do now. But who kept printing Bibles all those years? Who translated the Bible into 1400 languages? Who leads soul-winning revivals? Who risked death from diseases and cannibals to plant Christian missions worldwide? Not Armstrong!

Let us have some truth, for a change. Christ said (Matt. 16:18) "I will build my church and the gates of hell *shall not prevail* against it." Then His churches did NOT cease in 70 AD, or any other year. Acts 8:1 records "a great persecution against the church which was at Jerusalem" and that scattered the Christians elsewhere. The destruction of Jerusalem in 70 AD had the same effect. Christians went out into wider areas, preaching the gospel and starting new churches. If churches disappeared in some places, they started in others. The apostle John wrote his five books *after* 70 AD, and he warned against many heretics even then.

Like weeds, un-Christian sects and cults grow everywhere. They persist and proliferate. But Jesus said they could not destroy His real churches.

Armstrong, like Ishmael, is in constant warfare against those who are born again of the Spirit (John 3:5-8). "But as then he that was born of the flesh persecuted him that was born after the Spirit, even so it is now" (Gal. 4:29).

Armstrongites point their guns the wrong way. They pretend that 99% of Christendom is apostate and false, and that only their little crowd is the "true" church. But the NT tells of "multitudes" of true believers, in many places, while the apostates were comparatively few. Again, HLH and HWA reverse the road signs. The marks of apostasy and heresy describe Armstrongites well, but they point the finger at NT Christians.

Mr. Hoeh's myopic "history" omits the many heroic missionaries who went into Asia, Africa, Europe, the Americas, and savage islands. In spite of extreme dangers and persecutions, they won souls to Christ and started churches. Now that those places are safe, Armstrong moves in to plant tares.

Some Baptists—not all—believe that "Baptistic" churches have always existed since Christ's time. Among them were Novatians, Donatists, Paulicians, Lollards, Waldenses, and in every century Anabaptists. Dissenters from the Roman Catholic hierarchy existed in each century. The true gospel did survive. All of us now, including Armstrong, owe much to those faithful Christians whom HLH now vilifies.

Even in the Dark Ages, genuine Christians were also found in the Roman Catholic churches. Who can doubt that Bernard of Clairvaux (1091-1153) was one of God's choicest? Protestants love his beautiful hymn—

> Jesus, the very thought of Thee,
> With sweetness fills my breast;

But sweeter far Thy face to see,
And in Thy presence rest.

Yet Armstrong would relegate him to outer darkness, with all the rest of firm believers, many of whom suffered cruel martyrdom.

Martin Luther, admittedly not perfect, placed the world in his debt by his heroic stand against tyranny and apostasy. Who can count all schools, churches, hospitals, and missions built by Lutherans since then?

Episcopalians, with Church of England people, have enriched the world with their scholarship, hymns, and worldwide missionary work.

Presbyterians could cite many illustrious names of great preachers, scholars and missionaries. Their work in Korea has been wonderful.

Congregationalists have an illustrious history. They helped build our nation in its early days. They pioneered missionary work in Hawaii in 1820; my wife and I worshipped in their first church there in 1969.

And what of the Methodists, including George Whitefield? Their revivals saved England from the horrors of the French Revolution. Tens of thousands of people were genuinely saved to good works. Prison reforms started, child labor eased, labor laws improved, orphans cared for, many social service movements of later years trace their roots to the Wesleys, and their American circuit riders fought the good fight of faith valiantly.

Baptists take some pride in their missionary record, and in their growth worldwide from about 60,000 in 1792 to 31,400,000 in 1972.

The vast number of other denominations, Bible churches, independent churches, and Gospel churches all hold to full salvation now by simple faith in Christ. Their missionary zeal continues unabated. Praise the Lord!

As to the 200 or more Bible Institutes and colleges in the United States and Canada, perhaps the Moody Bible Institute in Chicago is best known. A constant stream of pastors, teachers, missionaries, evangelists, books, magazines, tracts, Christian films, missionary aviators, etc., flow annually from this great "West Point of Christian Service."

But Armstrong consigns them all to the devil! His plan is to *hinder* all this work of God. His own work consists of expanding his propaganda machines worldwide, the more to hamper soul-winning churches.

"Woe unto you, lawyers (Armstrongites)! For ye have taken away the key of knowledge; ye entered not in yourselves, and them that were entering in *ye hindered*" (Luke 11:52).

Imagine a "true" history of the "true" church omitting names as John Calvin, Martin Luther, John Wesley, Jonathan Edwards, Timothy Dwight, Charles Finney, Dwight L. Moody, Charles H. Spurgeon, Billy Sunday, Hudson Taylor, plus a host of other stalwarts. These were genuine believers who have enriched the world by their distinctly Christian labors.

All these wonderful servants of Christ, says Armstrong, have been deceiving the world. He has his head in a can! He reverses road signs. He calls evil good, and good evil. He quotes NT texts about false prophets and those verses fit Armstrong's writers snugly.

Armstrong claims originality, but he has borrowed heavily—without giving credits—from several older sects. He has the soul-sleep and sabbath and annihilation from the Adventists; downgrading of the Holy Spirit, denial of Christmas and Easter from Jehovah's Witnesses; British-Israelism from several such previous groups, and his "I shall be God" from Mormons. This list of purloined heresies is incomplete, but representative.

So what is new in Armstrongism? Mostly his cunning sales pitch. His unabashed arrogance. His slick paper, full color magazines. His "soft sell" approach, *pretending* not to work for converts, but pushing literature on prospects until they are hooked; then high pressure for funds! His imperial ecclesiastic machine needs worlds of money.

Any unbiased person, reading the NT, would not identify Armstrong's group with the churches described in the Acts or Epistles.

Yet Armstrong urges all Christians to withdraw from their own churches and join his (Hoeh, p. 29). He tries to steal sheep, to proselyte, and wreck good churches to build his own. He admits that he does not try to get unsaved people to be born again (NT preachers did), but he tries hard to hinder all churches that do win souls.

He is very suspicious of those who think for themselves. He orders his people NOT to gather without one of his own agents in charge. Christ trusted HIS followers; Armstrong does not. See Matthew 18:20.

In a personal letter to a friend an Armstrong official from Pasadena wrote, "the calling and mission of the Church is outlined in Matthew 24:14. Our job is to preach the Gospel of the coming Kingdom of God to the world as a witness. I am enclosing an article on what the Gospel of God is. Therefore, our job is to tell the world that Christ is going to return soon to establish the literal government of God on this earth."

This same letter admits, "we do not have any specific literature on organization, mission, and calling of God's (Armstrong's) church. Our organization is based on the Bible and specifically on such scriptures as 1 Corinthians 12:28 and Ephesians 4:11." (This is debatable.)

How strange, how incredible, that here is a man who boasts of having the only true church since 70 AD, that ALL others are wrong, and yet he has NO specific literature on the organization, mission, and calling of his church!

And yet he expects us to surrender our exceedingly rich heritage for his undefined, foggy, nebulous, amorphous, and indefinite "church."

But he does try to tell us what his "true" gospel is. Let us look at it, next. We want to read him carefully and treat him fairly.

15

ARMSTRONG'S "TRUE" GOSPEL TESTED

HERBERT W. ARMSTRONG (HWA) has a tract entitled, "What Is the True Gospel?" It is quite as vague and unscriptural as other writings by him and his staff.

As usual, HWA begins by accusing all non-Armstrongites of confusion, perplexity, divisions, and a "Babylon of disagreement."

Hoping to disarm his increasing number of critics, he wants Galatians 1:8, 9 to mean everyone but himself. But it fits him best of all. "But though we, or an angel from heaven, preach any other gospel unto you than that ye have received, let him be accursed. As we said before, so say I now again, If any man preach any other gospel unto you than that ye have received, let him be accursed."

Any similarity between the gospel Paul gave, and that of HWA, is quite accidental and incidental—and hardly recognizable. (If this seems harsh, Paul was much more so.)

Armstrong's "gospel" is a mere *announcement* of the future kingdom of God. It is simply advance news of the *future* earthly kingdom of "flesh and blood" (*Tomorrow's World*, January, 1970). His big verse is Matthew 24:14, "And this gospel of the kingdom shall be preached in all the world for a witness unto all nations; and then shall the end come." But this "gospel of the kingdom" is a *present-day* gospel, for a *present spiritual* kingdom. Matthew 5:3; 6:33; 12:28; 16:19 all show that the "gospel" of Matthew 24:14 is this same present-day gospel which saves sinners *now*.

Suppose a dying friend or relative asked you how to be saved. Would a news announcement about a future kingdom help him or satisfy him?

Suppose a drug addict asked you for the gospel. Would a future kingdom be any help in his present desperate condition? We do know that from five to ten times as many drug users are being saved—from drugs and other sins—by our old fashioned evangelism than by any other means.

When the Philippian jailer cried in desperation, "Sirs, what must I do to be saved?" did Paul read a news bulletin about a future kingdom?

No; this "kingdom of God" is a present reality. EVERY real Christian is in it NOW. The repentant thief entered the kingdom when he prayed. The Ethiopian entered the kingdom the instant he received Christ. Saul of Tarsus entered the kingdom on the Damascus Road, with instant salvation.

Of course we believe in the glorious future kingdom when Christ shall reign literally as King of kings and Lord of lords. But we also believe that we are saved NOW. We are in His kingdom the moment we believe, before we are baptized, and before we join a church.

HWA *fakes* 1 Corinthians 15:50, "Now this I say, brethren, that flesh and blood cannot inherit the kingdom of God; neither doth corruption inherit incorruption." The BODY of the repentant thief did not change, or inherit a kingdom. But his soul was instantly IN the kingdom of God, and shortly with Christ in paradise. "That which is born of flesh is flesh; and that which is born of spirit is spirit" (John 3:6). So our New Testament gospel says the new birth, and the kingdom, are for NOW.

The moment we believe we are delivered from the power of darkness, and "translated into the kingdom of his dear Son" (Col. 1:13). This is a present, enjoy-it-now experience for all who trust and obey Christ.

At the resurrection we shall receive new bodies, suited for the new kingdom, all in God's own time. It may be very soon.

We cannot speak for Roman Catholics, or for "liberals" who doubt or deny the gospel, but we do know what evangelicals believe and teach. We hold to the gospel as summarized by Paul in 1 Corinthians 15:1-4.

1. Moreover, brethren, I declare unto you *the gospel* which I preached unto you, which also ye have *received,* and in which ye *stand:*

2. By which also ye *are saved,* if ye keep in memory what I preached unto you, unless ye have believed in vain.

3. For I delivered unto you first of all that which I also received, that *Christ died for our sins* according to the scriptures;

4. And that he was *buried,* and that he *rose again* the third day according to the scriptures.

Isn't this exactly what evangelicals have been preaching for hundreds of years, with genuine conversions resulting? It surely is.

And does Paul's gospel here have *any* similarity to Armstrong's? HWA's is narrowed down and diluted to a mere notice of a future kingdom. We who are evangelicals have always included that too, but *salvation now* has priority because it is a prerequisite for the coming physical kingdom. In the Book of Acts, personal salvation was primary; everyone saved was *then* in the kingdom. This same kingdom was given in Acts 8:12; 14:22; 19:8; 20:25; 28:23, 31. But Armstrong's "gospel" is not there!

In HWA's tract, "What Do You Mean . . . Salvation?" he says on page 7 that the life we were born with is only temporary chemical existence. Then, to be kept saved, he says we must obey his laws. Referring to the Holy Spirit as "it," we must have "it" to be kept saved, he says.

Paul chided the Corinthians for their gullibility in accepting a gospel different from the one he preached, and for being "led astray from a sincere and pure devotion to Christ" (2 Cor. 11:3, 4).

The Armstrong "gospel" compels its victims to observe the Jewish sabbaths and feasts in order to keep whatever salvation they are allowed to have. But *not one verse* in the entire Bible commands a Gentile to keep the sabbaths. This alone brands HWA's "gospel" as false, spurious, untrue, deceitful, fraudulent, dishonest, and sly.

A friend wrote to Armstrongite Wilbur Berg:

"Believers in Jesus Christ who worship on Sunday are not judged, and will not be judged, for failing to keep the Jewish sabbath, or for neglecting the Jewish feast days, or for believing that Paul was correct when he said that Christ had done away with the need for observing old Jewish laws.

"No New Testament passage suggests that between conversion and the final judgment day, it is necessary to submit to Old Testament laws, to observe sabbath worship, or to keep Old Testament feast days."

Armstrong's emasculated, eviscerated "gospel" binds his followers to old Jewish laws and feasts, to dependence upon his legal system, to the status of a mere fetus instead of a truly born-again child of God. HWA offers a depersonalized "it" in place of the Holy Spirit, and total death until the resurrection. What a gloomy, sorry, substitute "gospel!"

The New Testament gospel is better. It is a gospel of peace (Eph. 6:15); the gospel of God (Rom. 1:1); the gospel of Christ (Rom. 1:16); the gospel of the *grace* of God (Acts 20:24); the gospel of salvation NOW (Eph. 1:13); and the glorious gospel of Christ—unseen by blinded people (2 Cor. 4:4).

To all Armstrongites Paul has a message: "I marvel that ye are so soon removed from him that called you into the grace of Christ unto another gospel, which is not another; but there are some that trouble you, and would pervert the gospel of Christ" (Gal. 1:6, 7).

Next, H. W. Armstrong asks "Why Were You Born?" We have the answer in the Bible.

16

WHY WERE YOU BORN?

A TRACT WITH the above title by H. W. Armstrong (HWA) says, here and elsewhere, that we are not saved when we receive Christ. This is "news" to millions of genuinely saved, happy, useful, sensible, Spirit-led Christian people. Salvation is three-fold: at converson we *were saved* from the penalty of sin; at present we *are being saved* from the power of sin; in the future we *shall be saved* from the presence of sin.

Of course, HWA wants to differ as much as possible from evangelical Christians, for that makes him and his followers seem superior.

His thinking here, as often elsewhere, is very faulty. For he argues that if a person is saved here and now, why doesn't God save him from present suffering? Why are his troubles not all ended?

The answer: we who are saved are here to carry out Christ's Great Commission (Matt. 28:18-20). We are to win as many souls to Christ as possible before we die. (HWA's antagonism hinders this work, Luke 11:52). We are never promised immunity from suffering in this life. Christ told His *saved* followers, "In the world ye shall have tribulation: but be of good cheer; I have overcome the world" (John 16:33; Phil. 1:29).

If every Christian were taken out of the world at the time of his conversion, who would be left to win the unsaved?

It seems incredible that HWA's "reasoning" could convince anyone.

HWA insists that if we accept the traditional view of the "fall of man," that then Satan is stronger than God. This we deny. "And though the wrong seems oft so strong, God is the Ruler yet" (M. D. Babcock).

On page 9 of HWA's pamphlet, "Why Were You Born," he implies that God *willed* Satan's invasion of the Garden of Eden to cause Adam's fall. But 2 Peter 3:9 says the Lord is "not willing that any should perish."

Also on page 9, HWA says Genesis does not tell of a completed creation. Yet Genesis 1:31 says, "And God saw everything he had made, and, behold, it was very good." And the next verse: "Thus the heavens and the earth were *finished,* and all the host of them."

HWA then insists that the earth's history of mankind will be only 6000 years. He holds to Ussher's chronology, but better scholars now know that the creation occurred long before 4004 BC. Yet many of HWA's "prophecies" depend on such Armstrong (and Ussher) errors.

HWA misunderstands 2 Peter 3:8, "one day is with the Lord as a thousand years, and a thousand years as one day." But this verse means that God's promises are as sure of fulfillment after 1000 years as after one day.

On his page 11, HWA quotes the King James Version of Ephesians 2:8, "By grace are ye saved through faith" and then on page 13 he compares this salvation to a baby *before its birth!* So HWA, who was born in 1892, is still a fetus! Not I, for the original Greek of Ephesians 2:8 is, "by grace you *have been saved* through faith."

HWA wrongly tries to show that good works are required for salvation, and this in spite of Ephesians 2:9, "not because of works, lest any man should boast." Of course we read v. 10 also, which says we are to do good works after we are saved.

HWA robs his followers of the great joys of *assurance* of salvation. He insists that the Bible says no one is yet saved, quoting Matthew 24:13. But this verse refers to a time yet future, something quite different.

Incredibly, on page 14 HWA says Christ was not perfect while on earth. Yet even His worst foes could find no fault in Him. So HWA is worse than Christ's enemies! Christ WAS perfect while on earth (John 1:14; 8:46; Heb. 7:26; 1 Peter 1:19; 1 John 3:5, etc.).

Blasphemy! On page 21 HWA boasts that at the resurrection he and his group will become Gods! He says this in bold capital letters. That is blasphemous. Or, is HWA's little god that small? And is this still more bait to lure people—and their tithes—to him for life?

He repeats this Satanic temptation on page 21, saying that those who follow him will actually be God, just like Jesus was and is. Compare Satan's temptation of Eve in Genesis 3:5, "ye shall be as God." But HWA bids more for your soul than Satan did; HWA omits "as" in *his* bid.

HWA seems to tempt people to follow Satan's example. For when Lucifer, through pride, sought to be like God he fell into terrible sin, thus becoming Satan, the devil. His fall is described in Isaiah 14:12-17 and Ezekiel 28:12-19. "How art thou fallen from heaven, O Lucifer . . . For thou hast said in thine heart, I will ascend into heaven, I will exalt my throne above the stars of God . . . I will be like the Most High . . .!"

And HWA tempts us to do likewise. HWA wants to be God! Jesus told such, "Ye are of your father the devil . . . he is a liar . . ." (John 8:44).

We could feel sorry for this poor deluded old man (HWA), and more so for his victims. They seem ignorant as to why they were born. They do not know the joys of being born again.

One wonders if HWA has *ever* been born again. He seems to deny such a possibility. We pray that he may be saved before it is too late.

17

ARE YOU A FETUS?
OR BORN AGAIN!

Dare to be true; nothing can need a lie;
A fault which needs it most, grows thereby.
—George Herbert

HERBERT W. ARMSTRONG (HWA) begins his tract, "What Do You Mean . . . Born Again?" as usual. He insinuates that all other writers on conversion are vague and mistaken. But better scholars than HWA have thought, spoken and written about being "born again" for centuries—all with great profit to millions of genuine Christians.

Armstrong's fantastic views on conversion may have inspired a cartoon in *Christianity Today* (8-27-71). It showed Paul talking to the Philippian jailer. Paul said, "What must you do to be saved? That's an interesting question. Is your concern existential, ecumenical, eschatological, or evangelistic?" HWA's concern is proselyting and unbiblical.

HWA resorts to facetious ridicule in suggesting that "giving one's heart to the Lord" involves opening the chest to remove an actual heart. Every Bible reader knows that "heart" represents one's entire life. It does so in nearly 1,000 Bible verses.

In his third paragraph, HWA represents himself as the first and only person who knows what the Bible says or means. Such egotism! Yet in his 1969 *Envoy*, p. 305, he wrote that he had "found the way of humility, exalting God instead of vanity, exalting the self."

111

He says "even preachers" are deceived. But those who preach the "born again" doctrine, as New Testament preachers did, have won millions of true converts who are the salt of the earth and the lights of the world. HWA's converts are converted to HWA, to a mere man, and to a cult that fights faithful churches and pastors. It does little else.

As to the phrase, "Born again," HWA assumes superiority by saying that we who use the phrase have not the least conception of its meaning. But *we do know.* Hundreds of millions of Christians *know* they have passed "from darkness to light, and from the power of Satan to God" (Acts 26:18).

In denying this precious, transforming, Biblical experience of the New Birth, HWA calls it a diabolical conspiracy on mankind, beginning at about 50 A.D. Such is his prelude to declaring flatly that he, HWA himself, has made the greatest discovery of this century! *HWA* says so!

After berating Bible preachers, HWA finally unveils his earth-shaking "incredible" discovery and revelation by distorting 1 John 3:9, "Whosoever is born of God doth not commit sin; for his seed remaineth in him, and he cannot sin, because he is born of God." HWA thinks this means a born-again person finds it impossible to sin; therefore, he postpones the new birth until the resurrection.

But the new birth means an *added nature,* the divine nature, given to the converted person, so that he now has *two* natures. The old one is called "flesh" and the new is "spirit" (John 3:6; Gal. 5:16, 17). It is this *new* nature that cannot sin, because it is from God. It is "His seed" or progeny from God that cannot sin. The *old* nature can sin (1 John 1:8, 10).

Every Christian knows about this internal conflict between his old sinful nature and the new divine nature. But does HWA know it?

Next, HWA says Christ could have sinned; otherwise, why was He tempted? We could say, He was tempted to show that He could NOT sin. And He is the same today, yesterday, and forever (Heb. 13:8); if He could have sinned on earth, then why not now? And He IS God—who cannot sin (Heb. 6:18; Titus 1:2). So HWA fails again and again.

HWA says that "born again" does not refer to conversion. But the experience of being born again IS conversion and regeneration. Items—

This new birth is not from man but of God (John 1:13; 1 Peter 1:3).

None can enter heaven without being born again (John 3:3, 5).

This new birth is given by the Holy Spirit (John 3:6; Titus 3:5).

The new birth, symbolized by baptism is real newness of life (Rom. 6:4).

The new nature is called "the inward man" (Rom. 7:22; 2 Cor. 4:16).

All believers are now born again (Rom. 8:16, 17; 1 Peter 2:2; 1 John 5:1).

Gospel preaching is the good instrument in evangelism (1 Cor. 4:15).

The new creation is very real to us (2 Cor. 5:17; Gal. 6:15; Eph. 2:10).

Solid evidence of new birth in Christians now (Eph. 2:1, 5; Col. 2:12; 3:1).

New birth is a divine creation, a new man, sure of heaven (Eph. 4:24).

The new birth is based on the Word of God (James 1:18; 1 Peter 1:23).

Being born again, we partake of the divine nature NOW (2 Peter 1:4).

Every one of these good verses has the new birth in this life, *now,* before the resurrection. HWA is directly contrary to the Bible. More, this present new birth produces likeness to God (Eph. 4:24; Col. 3:10), likeness to Christ (Rom. 8:29; 2 Cor. 3:18; 1 John 3:2), knowledge of God (Col. 3:10), hatred of sin (1 John 3:9; 5:18), victory over the world (1 John 5:4), and delight in God's Word (Rom. 7:22).

Some evidences of this new birth *now:* faith in Christ (1 John 5:1), righteousness (1 John 2:29), and brotherly love (1 John 4:7).

With such overwhelming proofs of HWA being wrong on the new birth, one has to suspect him of evil motives. Does he want to destroy assurance of salvation in order to make people dependent upon himself? This seems to be true in several of his misleading articles.

"The human heart, unaided, will not invent exact opposites of Christian teaching" (Kirby Kinman, a pastor who has studied demonism). Anyone teaching so many opposites of Christianity, as HWA does, must have been influenced by Satan somehow, sometime, somewhere.

HWA attempts to use the Greek in order to prove himself right and all preachers wrong. Mistakenly, he says the Greek *gennao* is the only word used for "begotten" and "born." What about *palingenesias* in Titus 3:5, *anagegennemenoi* in 1 Peter 1:23, *apekuesen* in James 1:18, or *ktisthentes* in Ephesians 2:10?

Mistakenly, HWA differentiates between "begotten" and "born" but each word implies the other. All the "begots" in Matthew 1:2-16 certainly mean births as well! In spite of this, HWA misreads 1 Corinthians 4:15 to mean that the Corinthian Christians were begotten but not yet born as such! But Paul called them all sanctified, saints, and a *new* creation.

Utterly impossible and dishonest is HWA's bald assertion that Christ was not born of God until His resurrection. He quotes Romans 1:4 as his proof(?) but that good verse says no such thing.

And HWA uses John 3:6 wrongly, "That which is born of the flesh is flesh; and that which is born of the Spirit is Spirit." This means that when one becomes a Christian he then has two natures—flesh and spirit—at the same time. HWA says we must wait until we die and are resurrected before we can be born of the Spirit! He goes to incredible lengths to make himself different from us. Perhaps he is; he may not be born again.

So now he says a convert to Christ is *only a fetus*, and that he will remain so until the resurrection. But not one verse in the Bible calls us a fetus, or implies it, or even suggests such a grotesque concept.

No census bureau will count fetuses. Yet those born again were numbered (Acts 2:41; 4:4, etc.).

A human fetus remains so for about nine months. But the repentant thief was born again a few hours before his death, while great Christians like George Mueller and Fanny Crosby lived wonderfully useful lives about 80 years each. A "fetus" may be twins or even quintuplets!

The Christians in the New Testament are described as walking, running, speaking, working, etc. How can a fetus do such work?

Where in the Bible is the Christian's resurrection called a new birth?

HWA admits a fetus has no "mental maturity" but the writers of the New Testament were mature mentally and spiritually.

HWA mistakenly says the Greek word for "adoption" in Romans 8:15 should be "spirit of sonship." He errs twice; he concedes sonship here but he denies it elsewhere, and he mistranslates *huiothesias* which means adoption, or "placing as sons."

HWA errs again by saying a Christian is begotten spiritually when he is baptized. Not so; baptism never begat or saved anyone; it is not magic; it never procures or secures salvation. It should follow conversion.

Never is the new birth dependent upon the resurrection of the body.

Instead, being born again is a *present* experience. "Everyone that loveth *is* born of God (1 John 4:7). "For whatsoever *is* born of God overcometh the world" (1 John 5:4). "We know that whosoever *is* born of God sinneth not" (1 John 5:18). And yet HWA prates against "these deceived people" who witness like this about their born-again experiences.

Not surprisingly, HWA denies the Trinity. (See our chapter 25.)

HWA denies what millions of Spirit-filled, intelligent, God-called Christians *know* as their new birth. I know it too. As a teenager, one wonderful April 30, I confessed my sins and then trusted Christ to save me. He did! That very day. I was born again. I received a new nature from God. Then I had two natures, the old and the new; I still have. The old will disappear at death, or at Christ's return. The new nature is immortal, eternal, glorious—for me as with millions of other believers.

So this, Mr. Armstrong, is what we mean by being born again. We think if you knew its joy you would write differently than you do. But we will have patience and hear you further, comparing your words with our Bibles.

> Blessed assurance, Jesus is mine!
> Oh, what a foretaste of glory divine!
> Heir of salvation, purchase of God,
> Born of His Spirit, Washed in His blood.
>
> This is my story, this is my song,
> Praising my Savior all the day long.
> —Fanny J. Crosby

18

FALSE CONVERSION --
A MORTAL DANGER

Even more vitriolic than most Armstrong writers is Roderick C. Meredith (RCM) who wrote a tract with the above title.

His violent attacks on good pastors violate God's Word in Psalm 105:15, "Touch not mine anointed, and do my prophets no harm."

His psychological wiles are hypnotic. Armstrong's strategists seem to work on the theory that the more they insult their prospects, the more likely naive people are to believe Armstrongism. By feeding resentment against pastors whose honest preaching exposes their sins, such people transfer all Armstrong's insults toward those faithful ministers. Such attacks on preachers make one feel superior!

It does seem that Armstrongites have fallen into a theological mud hole. They have an endless supply of "mud" to throw at Christians.

Mr. Meredith's first two columns (two of nine) are spent in accusing us of almost total ignorance, religious babylon, hate-to-admit-we-were-wrong, lacking something vital, blinded, wholly deceived, spiritually drunk, stupidly satisfied, confidence misplaced, dangerously deceived, empty, falsely converted, personal vanity, confused, et cetera.

All this abuse is meant to "condition" us into discovering how much we need Armstrong's cure for all these ills! He wants desperately for us to think we have never been converted; that all gospel preachers are stupid and blinded, and that our only hope is in Armstrong's new panacea.

So what is real conversion, according to Armstrongism?

It is, says RCM, to be led by the Holy Spirit. But is this news? "By their fruits ye shall know them," Jesus said. The fruit of the Spirit is love—but where is love in the vicious name-calling of RCM?

We have before shown that the worldwide fruits of evangelical Christians are just the same as those of Christ and His apostles. In contrast, what is the fruit of Armstrongism? Only more propaganda that is anti-church, anti-Christian, anti-Spirit, and contrary to Scripture.

Armstrongites actually deny the Personality of the Holy Spirit, thus proving they do not know Him, much less His good first fruit of love. They join the blasphemous "God-is-dead" people when they *kill* the Personhood of the Holy Spirit.

Not knowing the *first* thing about the Holy Spirit, how can they know anything about real conversion? For it is the Holy Spirit who converts us (John 3:5, 6, 8), and they depersonalize Him; they take the life out of Him. How, then, can their "conversion" be anything but false?

And of course Armstrongites make the Ten Commandments, especially the sabbath, their criteria. We have shown in our chapter four their blunder in misreading 2 Corinthians 3:6-17. We may repeat some of this.

Mr. RCM implies that baptism is necessary for salvation (we admit it is needed for obedience). But not one Bible verse demands baptism before conversion. The repentant thief on the cross and Saul of Tarsus were saved without baptism, though Saul was baptized as soon as possible.

Real conversion comes instantly to anyone who will confess his sins to God, trusting in Christ's death on the cross and His resurrection to save him from the penalty of his sins. One must receive Christ as *Lord,* obey Him conscientiously, and then continue in the faith.

What Armstrongites mean by being led of the Spirit is full submission to all of Armstrong's rules, dictates, and legalistic observances as the sabbaths and Jewish feasts. But Armstrong is not the Holy Spirit.

The thief repenting on the cross received instant salvation.

Just so, when anyone prays sincerely, "Lord, be merciful to me, a sinner," that moment salvation is his. Isn't this Good News compared to Armstrongism?

And Armstrong's RCM does not give the plan of salvation. Instead, he asks all prospects to write for "help" from one of their trained and cunning propagandists, drilled and brainwashed in a college maintained for that purpose. This agent, if successful, will then guide one further into the tentacles of Armstrongism, after which the financial pressure begins. They want ten per cent of one's income, and then another ten per cent for their Jewish feasts. More, they urge their members to borrow additional money from banks to finance HWA's expensive propaganda.

And even though Armstrongism is only one of 70 or more such "isms" that have sprung up since Christ, they say theirs is the only right one.

They do seem confused, especially on conversion. No wonder one well informed Christian, Mr. Roger F. Campbell, said that Herbert W. Armstrong should be called "Mr. Confusion."

Now let us see what Garner Ted Armstrong (son of HWA), the radio speaker, writer, and likely successor to the throne, has to say about Repentance.

19

MY LETTER TO
GARNER TED ARMSTRONG

On February 26, 1971, I wrote to Mr. G. T. Armstrong.

I have just read your tract, "What Is Real Repentance?" It raises some real questions and suspicions.

You suggest that all present church members are only "religious" and that without your beliefs they are not genuine.

You say, correctly, that many decisions made in mass evangelism do not last long. On the other hand, many such decisions DO last.

You omit John the Baptist who first preached the gospel and won a great many souls to Christ in mass evangelism. Christ and the Apostles endorsed the Baptist's message, his theology and his baptism.

What *did* Christ require of the repentant thief on the cross in addition to his simple prayer of receiving Jesus as his Lord? Nothing.

As to having the Spirit of Christ, see Luke 9:49-56 where Christ rebuked those (like you) who thought only they were right and all others were wrong. You imply that no church but yours has the Spirit of Christ.

"All is vanity" you say (Eccl. 1:2). But Solomon wrote *that* while he was a backslider, "under the sun," and thus apart from God. The Bible, conversion, missions, churches, and dedicated Christians are not vanity. Vanity is like your pride in boasting that you alone have the true gospel.

To be liked by others is mostly commendable. You want it too!

"Ensnared in Society"—by this you seem to include our good churches. But Christ loved the church and gave Himself for it. He gave His life for the Twelve and some of them were not so good. Why should we not give ourselves for our churches now, instead of to your group?

You say that Jesus calls us OUT of society, but He said for us to be "the salt of the earth" (Matt. 5:13-16). We can be in the world but not of it. We are told to go into all the world with His gospel.

You say if one is a true Christian, his former friends and relatives will hate him? Are you sure? The boy Jesus grew "in favor with man" (Luke 2:52). John the Baptist had the respect of "all the people" (Luke 20:6). The early Christians had "favor with all the people" (Acts 2:47). We are told to give "no offense" (2 Cor. 6:3).

One's own family will "look down" on him? Do you say this in order to have your prospects follow you? "A man's foes . . . of his own household" because of Christ or because of you?

If one really follows Christ, his relatives will persecute him? Oh, to be a martyr—for Armstrong! How? get your loved ones to hate you! Then you have proof that you are a *real* Christian! This is an old trick. The Jehovah's Witnesses used it many years. And Joe Smith was killed (unfortunately) and so he was a martyr—*then* some gullible people followed his polygamous teaching. If a cult makes one obnoxious, does that make the cult right?

To come out of "this society" seems to imply, come out from your own good church and get into the Armstrong crowd.

It costs one's life to be a Christian. Right. My life for Christ, but not for Armstrong.

To lay down one's life for Christ is very good, but your subtle implication is, lay down your life for Armstrong. We already HAVE laid down our lives for Christ.

"After repenting"—but repenting IS a conversion, a change of mind, the new birth. Bible repentance *means* salvation. Thus, Acts 2:38 means to repent is to be saved. Then baptism followed.

Is the Holy Spirit "implanted" after baptism? Not so with Cornelius and his household who received the Spirit before their baptism. Paul was saved three days before his baptism.

Not one person in the world was told to depend on his baptism for salvation. Water can not save anyone; the precious blood of Christ does that (1 Peter 1:19; Rev. 1:5).

If anyone trust in "works" of any kind for his salvation, then he has "fallen from grace" (Gal. 5:4), and Christ "has become of no effect."

"Keep the laws of God"—does this mean all Jewish laws? "Anciently, a man brought a lamb. . ." This was God's law, too, but do you obey it now? No.

"Baptizing Counsel" for those who want to repent? So—is there no other way to be saved and baptized but to ask your agent to come into our homes? No; you do not ask to come, but how could a hint be any stronger? When you teach that only you have the plan of salvation, and real baptism, and that *our souls depend on you*—of course you expect us to invite you. Clever salesmanship! This is how you "creep into houses" (2 Tim. 3:6; Jude 4).

Your men (only) are fully qualified to EXPLAIN the Bible, you say. But you don't even explain real repentance in your lengthy tract. *How did anyone ever get saved before your group came along?*

NOTHING TO SELL, is your boast. But you HAVE! Items—

1. You "compass sea and land to win one proselyte" for Armstrong.

2. You imply that only Armstrong is the voice of God. No others.

3. You imply that to suspect Armstrong is to doubt God!

4. You expect us to forsake our good churches for Armstrong.

5. You expect us to disobey Christ who said, "A stranger will they *not* follow, but will flee from him" (John 10:5).

6. Once hooked, you expect your followers to send their tithes and offerings to your headquarters. How else is your propaganda paid for? Once your prospect depends on your system for salvation, *of course* he will pay and *pay* and PAY. Your experience PROVES that.

7. Nothing to sell? Only *lifelong dependence* on Armstrong for soul security. What a clever deal!

8. "Nothing to sell"—the cunningest advertising gimmick ever known.

9. To "buy" Armstrong one must read his Bible through *his*

colored glasses, for only he has the "RIGHT" way! All OTHERS are wrong! (End of letter)

No reply has come, in these many months.

But Armstrong's presses keep on producing pollution. Therefore, we must continue exposing some more of his misleading material. Next is the old "second chance" heresy, pushed so long by Jehovah's Witnesses, and now peddled by the Armstrongites.

✿ ✿ ✿

In recent years Armstrong's magazines have less anti-church propaganda and more colorful articles of general interest. Some of these articles have good material, and thus are good bait for the unwary.

✿ ✿ ✿

FLASH! The Evangelical Press News Service, 4-1-72 Reports "Herbert W. Armstrong's son reportedly 'in the bonds of Satan' " and "Garner Ted Armstrong, number two man in the empire built by H. W. Armstrong, is reportedly out of favor with the Lord and with his father."

The *Los Angeles Times,* 4-1-72, headlines—"Garner Ted Armstrong Reported in Disfavor. Son of Founder of Worldwide Church of God Replaced in Key Jobs, Sources Say."

The Seattle *Post-Intelligencer,* 4-1-72, Earl Hansen, religion editor, said he was able to confirm at a Seattle service that Garner Ted had confessed he was "in the bonds of Satan."

Herbert W. Armstrong, 3-24-72, announced that his two magazines would be combined into one. This "will reduce the expenditure . . . . by a considerable sum," he says.

June, 1972—Garner Ted came back to broadcasting Armstrongism.

20

IS SALVATION POSSIBLE
AFTER DEATH?

"Is THIS THE Only Day of Salvation?" is a tract by Armstrongite C. Paul Meredith (CPM). He implies by the question form that other future "days of salvation" may exist. His title is an obvious reference to 2 Corinthians 6:2, "Behold, now is the accepted time; behold, now is the day of salvation." CPM wants it to read, "now is *a* day of salvation."

The Revised Standard Version has it, "now is *the* day . . ." Similarly, the American Standard, Weymouth, Montgomery, Amplified, Confraternity Versions all have it, "now is the day of salvation."

The Williams: "right now it is the day of salvation."

Living Letters: "Today He is ready to save you."

Phillips: "This very day is the day of salvation."

Good News for Modern Man: "Today is the day to be saved."

New English Bible: "Now, I say, has the day of deliverance dawned."

But all Armstrongites want it to read "A day" instead of "THE day." If that were allowed, then the first phrase (now is the accepted time) would lose its meaning. For Paul was always urgent in pressing gospel demands in the present. He held out no hope for a "second chance" later. Armstrong copies the Jehovah's Witnesses in this "second chance" theory.

They say the Greek of 2 Corinthians 6:2 has no article before "day"; that it could read, "now is (a) day of salvation. To be technical—

Sometimes with a noun which the context proves to be definite the article is not used. This places stress upon the qualitative aspect of the noun rather than its mere identity. An object of thought may be conceived of from two points of view: as to *identity* or *quality*. To convey the first point of view the Greek uses the article; for the second the anarthrous construction is used." (from Dana & Mantey's *Manual Grammar of the Greek New Testament*, p. 149)

The Armstrongites do not seem concerned about the salvation of lost sinners now. They think people will have a better chance (their first?) to be saved "at the great white throne judgment" of Revelation 20:11–15. Mr. CPM, on page 8 of his tract, says as much, with NO basis whatever. Mr. CPM holds out *entirely false hopes* of salvation in Revelation 20. No hope for a first, second, or third chance is in those verses.

So Armstrongism (1) offers only false hopes for the future; (2) gives no real gospel of full salvation now; (3) tries hard to hinder evangelistic persons and churches from their blessed task of soul winning.

Isn't that exactly what the devil wants?

Errors flourish in Armstrong's writings. In *Tomorrow's World*, July, 1971, page 15, a Mr. Wiedenheft says that during Christ's ministry on earth, not one person was converted! Mary Magdalene was, for out of her Christ had cast seven demons (Mark 16:9). Zacchaeus was; "Jesus said unto him, This day is salvation come to this house . . . For the Son of man is come to seek and to *save that which was lost*" (Luke 19:9, 10). "Jesus made and baptized more disciples (converts) than John" (John 4:1). The repentant thief on the cross was soundly converted (Luke 23:40–43).

As to those who have never heard of Christ, CPM says they have never had a chance to be saved. He ignores Romans 1:20.

He *blames God* for "blinding" people in order that they would keep on sinning and suffer the consequences (p. 6). He also says that out of love and wisdom (?), God blinds people who now reject the truth, in order that they will sin still more and thus learn their lesson more thoroughly! Thus he blames God for what he *says* we are now—stupidly satisfied, insipid and inane, spiritually drunk, etc.

One of CPM's headlines shouts that Christ did not try to

convert everyone. Then why did Christ come at all? And what does Luke 19:10 mean?

On page 6, CPM says Christ did not try to disturb people's spiritual blindness. But He *did!* Luke says so, Luke 11:37-52; 13:3-5; 15:3-32; 18:18-24. John says so, John 5:34, 37-40, 44-47; 8:12-19; 10:22-39.

Has any of Armstrong's writers ever produced *one* new spiritual truth that helps anybody? Have they given *one* idea which was not taken from some previous cult? A friend wrote to CPM 8-30-71, "How poverty-stricken the world was in theological truth before Mr. Armstrong appeared!"

On page 7 of CPM's tract, he takes 2 Peter 2:1, 2 which fits *his* kind like a glove, but which he aims at all evangelical preachers. Now I have known hundreds of faithful, Biblical, fruitful, intelligent, soul winning preachers in a long lifetime, and NOT ONE has "secretly brought in destructive heresies" and NOT ONE has denied "the Lord that bought them."

It is Armstrong's meetings that are secret, where destructive heresies are taught (I heard some), where the Lord's words are denied, where false teachers abound, and where the devil's work of hindering the gospel is done.

Mr. CPM says it is no stigma or disgrace to evangelicals that they are "blinded now!" But Armstrong attempts with the most slanderous words to shame and vilify everyone who is not in his church.

On page 8, Mr. CPM says that those not converted by Armstrong's formula have been "blinded by God." Then if there is "no stigma or disgrace" to those non-Armstrongites who are so blinded by God, then such stigma and disgrace must be transferred to God who, says CPM, is responsible for our "religious error," our being "completely deceived," our being "spiritually drunk," and our being "insipid and inane."

Again on page 8, CPM says the people of ancient Tyre and Sidon will get their "first chance" to be saved after their resurrection. Christ did not say that, nor does any verse in the Bible. In fact, Revelation 22:11 says, "He that is unjust, let him be unjust still."

It seems the Armstrong people are greatly displeased with the great number of people and churches of all denominations who are trying to win souls to Christ now. But we have orders from

Christ, not from Armstrong, to win all we can (Matt. 28:18 20). The Book of Acts has 20 imperatives, telling unbelievers to repent and be saved.

The Armstrong people try to hinder evangelistic churches (by attacking and proselyting from us), and thus stop our soul winning which is like "pulling them out of the fire" (Jude 23). Like snipers shooting at fire department men who are trying to save property and lives from fires, so Armstrong's agents snipe at evangelical Christians.

"Behold, *now* is the day of salvation." Let us always use the plain words of Scripture as guidelines, even as we must point out additional fallacies in Armstrongism. Fortunately, and mercifully, we can be brief on most of them, especially on baptism—a subject on which this author has written several books.

21

ARMSTRONG'S BAPTISM EXAMINED

GARNER TED ARMSTRONG, son of H. W., writes on "Should You Be Baptized?" He begins with typical scornful sarcasm. He assumes to describe an evangelist in Brooklyn, New York, "panting, perspiring" and screaming. Dozens rush up for baptism—by being sprayed with a fire hose!

This stupid story is obviously a very rare exception or facetious fiction. Incredible. It shows how far, in desperation, Armstrong (GTA) will go to downgrade others. It reveals lack of respect for the intelligence of their followers to think they would believe such ridicule.

I have witnessed, and shared, many street meetings but never anything as impossible as GTA pretends to describe. But by such silly "straw men" GTA and his ilk prepare their followers for more impossible fantasies.

GTA describes an immersion in "waterproof costumes" but never in many years of observation, experience, and reading have I seen such a thing.

And, monotonously, GTA accuses others of the confusion *which is his.*

GTA refers to Matthew 24:4, 5, 11 where Christ warns us of false prophets. We have proved in *scores* of cases that the Armstrongs are both false prophets and false historians. Yet by their psychological cunning they have led their followers to accept their voices as the voice of God.

GTA refers to the 400 or so differing groups of Christians in the Western world, evidently intending by this inflated number to show how many are inferior to his own. But Armstrongism is a late comer among the 70 or more cults arising since apostolic times.

GTA errs again when he says that Christ said the great majority of churches would be wrong. He fails to cite chapter and verse. He can't.

But GTA says one sensible thing: he advises his readers not to believe him without checking on him by the Bible. We have done exactly that, and *we do not* believe him. But we know, as GTA knows, that many readers will not, or can not, check up on him. Many half-truths, more deceptive than outright lies, will induce careless readers to accept Armstrongism.

Since I have studied baptism considerably, I know that GTA is in serious error. His *mode* of baptism can be correct, but if his *motive* is wrong, then he is terribly wrong. And his motive IS wrong. For nowhere does the Bible say that baptism produces a "new" person. Baptism is not magic; it is not a rabbit's foot, or a fetish, charm, or amulet. Baptism never regenerated anybody; only the Holy Spirit can do that.

John the Baptist refused to baptize certain Pharisees and Sadducees who came to his baptism. They had to repent (be converted) first, confessing their sins. Likewise, I have refused to baptize anyone who could not show good evidence of conversion.

But John baptized genuine converts—saved people—immediately; so did the apostles. At Pentecost, 3000 converts were baptized right *after* their conversion. The Ethiopian was baptized as soon as he believed in Christ as his Savior. Cornelius and his household were baptized as soon as they believed, but the Holy Spirit filled them before their baptism. The Philippian jailer was baptized "the same hour of the night" as his conversion. Always, salvation preceded baptism. Never did baptism produce salvation. For baptism is pictorial, not procurative; it is symbolic and not sacramental or saving.

In spite of hundreds of thousands of evangelical, intelligent, trained pastors, GTA still implies that only his Ambassador college agents can baptize properly. But where did they get their authority?

Who baptized the first Armstrongites? If all Christians previous to H. W. Armstrong were wrong, and devil worshippers, how could HWA and/or GTA ever have correct baptism? Is not theirs a spurious baptism?

With Armstrongism claiming its origin on January 7, 1934, how and where was their baptism secured?

Is their baptism self-authorized? Then it is false. Is it from some non-Armstrong people? Then the *Armstrongs* must admit it is false!

Here is a dilemma for all Armstrongites. Either they have no real baptism, or they are compelled to trace their own baptism to some group which they now ascribe to Satan.

To trust in Armstrongism is like clinging to a broken reed. "Lo, thou trustest in the staff of this broken reed, on Egypt on which, if a man lean, it will go into his hand, and pierce it" (Isa. 36:6).

As we continue reading Armstrongism, it seems to grow weaker and weaker. Let us now see if Junior Armstrong is right on the church.

22

SHOULD YOU JOIN
A CHURCH?

IN THIS TRACT, Garner T. Armstrong (GTA) again complains about the hundreds of differing groups of Christians. Strange, with so many, he could not find one good enough for him! And his father started one more, packed with more confusion than any others. They are brazen and bold in saying that all previous groups are wrong. The Armstrongs, only, have the plain truth! "Incredible."

Where is the psychological trick here? Is it in numbers? If GTA had mentioned only ten other groups, then his own would be superior to only ten. But he says 400; therefore, his group has greatly increased stature by being superior (?) to so very many.

Candidly, I have taught Bible, theology, and ecclesiology in seminary, college, pulpits, and Sunday Schools for 50 years. I have read a great many Armstrong tracts, with Scripture references to learn what they teach. And I know how terribly wrong, hurtful, unreasonable, illogical and disordered Armstrongism is.

Incredibly, GTA tries to tell us that his is the right church on the basis of Luke 12:32, "Fear not, little flock; for it is your Father's good pleasure to give you the kingdom." Then he said the "true church" will be hated, and GTA wants his followers to believe that this *proves* Armstrongism is the true church. But the early church (over 3000) had "favor with all the people" (Acts 2:47).

The Armstrongs say the New Testament always says the "true church" would be a small one. But *only once* is this even hinted, and that to the Twelve only (Luke 12:22, 32). On the other hand—

Acts 4:32 "And the *multitude* of those that believed. . ."

Acts 5:14 "And believers were the more added to the Lord, *multitudes*. . ."

Acts 5:16 "There came also a *multitude* out of the cities. . ."

Acts 6:2 "Then the Twelve called the *multitude* of the disciples. . ."

Acts 6:7 "the number of the disciples multiplied in Jerusalem *greatly;* and a *great* company of the priests were obedient to the faith."

Acts 4:4 "But *many* . . . believed . . . of the men about 5000. . . ."

Acts 9:31 "Then had the churches rest . . . were edified . . . *multiplied*."

Acts 11:21 "And a *great number* believed, and turned to the Lord."

Acts 12:25 "But the word of God grew and *multiplied*. . . ."

Acts 13:45 "But when the Jews saw the *multitudes*. . . ."

Acts 14:1 "A great *multitude* . . . Jews and Greeks . . . believed."

Acts 15:30 "When they had gathered the *multitude* together. . . ."

Acts 17:4 "And some of them believed . . . a great *multitude*. . . ."

Revelation 17:9; 19:6 "a great *multitude*, which no man could number."

"Multitudes" are mentioned in the four gospels 68 times. Yet GTA implies that because his group is "weak and little" that it only is right.

He says very few attend their church because it is right in its beliefs! And he implies that only his is right; all others are counterfeit. His is the ONE church on this globe preaching the one true gospel. GTA says so! He also says his is the only church preaching on prophecy; he is wrong. Sermons on prophecy have been preached a good deal in evangelical churches for many years, even before GTA was born.

GTA implies that at Pentecost Peter did not tell the baptized converts to join a church. But Acts 2:41 says, "the same day there were *added* unto them about three thousand souls." And Acts 2:47, "And the Lord *added* to the church daily such as should be saved."

Walking forward in church on the pastor's invitation to surrender to Christ and join a church is one good way to obey the Lord (Matt. 10:32). But GTA fires away at almost any convenient target; he wants his prospects to find as many faults with their pastors and churches as possible.

"Now I beseech you, brethren, mark them who cause divisions and offenses contrary to the doctrine which ye have learned, and avoid them. For they that are such serve not our Lord Jesus Christ but their own belly, and by good words and fair speeches deceive the hearts of the innocent" (Rom. 16:17, 18).

"I would they were even cut off who trouble you" (Gal. 5:12).

Armstrongism troubles many people. It is so dogmatic, so confident, so wrong, so arrogant, so cocksure. And most pastors of our churches have not taught their people how to discern between Bible truths and such deceitfulness as the many cults promote so persistently.

"If you fool with a snake at all, kill it," was the advice a Methodist pastor gave some years ago. In following that counsel we must continue to show how heretical, how divisive, how erroneous, and how deceitful this Armstrong cult really is. This task is not pleasant, but it is now very needful.

Then let us see how they deal with the Lord's Supper.

23

ARMSTRONG'S CONFUSING COMMUNION

Mr. H. W. ARMSTRONG begins discussing the Lord's Supper by downgrading all churches but his own. Can he not present his case without attacking those Christians who have a long and creditable history of faithfulness to the work and precious Word of God?

So Mr. Armstrong (HWA) says that the Lord's Supper, in common with many other vital parts of Bible doctrine, has stumbled into the mire of erring traditions. It could be that HWA is himself in a deep ditch, and that his viewpoint is muddied and distorted for that reason.

HWA says the first Lord's Supper occurred after sundown, but no verse says so. It was in "the evening" (Matt. 26:20).

And HWA says that foot washing was commanded. But this was not made an ordinance; it has no reference to the death and resurrection of Christ as baptism and communion have; it did teach humility and service which can now be taught more effectively otherwise; it was a needful service *then* when people wore sandals and walked in much dust; it is not now of *any* service to anyone. Surely, foot-washing people are careful to come with their feet already clean! Stockings, too, of whatever length are now worn but such are never mentioned in the Bible. The "hosen" of Daniel 3:21 was a "fine upper garment."

HWA says communion was observed once a year, at Passover time. But better scholars than HWA believe it was observed weekly at first, though the frequency is not prescribed for us.

Armstrongism is tenacious for Jewish feasts. But "the observance of all such feasts, such as the Passover, the Feast of Unleavened Bread, the Feast of Tabernacles, and Pentecost, being symbolic, ceased at the cross, and *Christians should not observe them*" (from a Seventh Day Adventist tract, "The Passover Abolished," August, 1954).

When such feasts are mentioned in the Acts and Epistles, they are calendar dates to identify time, and carry *no* command for us to observe them. Paul did notice them for a time—in order to win Jews to Christ. Each day has its own meaning for certain people, and July Fourth would mean little or nothing to an alien in the United States. The Jewish feasts were "shadows" of the Christ who came as the living reality (Col. 2:17; Heb. 8:5; 10:1). *No Gentile* was ever commanded to keep Jewish feasts.

Now as to Acts 20:7, "when the disciples came together to break bread." HWA says this means ordinary, daily meals. But then—had they fasted all of the six previous days, until "the first day of the week?" Of course not. HWA here is anxious to avoid a Sunday meeting and Communion; to do so he must interpose a six-day fast, only to dodge the truth.

And he says that to "break bread" is NEVER used to mean the Lord's Supper in the New Testament. But see 1 Corinthians 10:16, "The bread which we break, is it not the communion of the body of Christ?" And 1 Corinthians 11:23, 24, ". . . took bread . . . he broke it." Jesus took bread, and blessed it, and broke it (Matt. 26:26; Mark 14:22; Luke 22:19).

* * *

One wonders if Armstrong's writers ever studied Hermeneutics, the science of Bible interpretation. (I taught it many years.) They seem to break most of the recognized rules in promoting their errors.

"Twelve Rules for Bible Study" is a tract by David Jon Hill (DJH). Not surprisingly, he suggests that all but his group misunderstand, twist, distort, malign, misrepresent, and lie about the Bible!

Such a great scholar as James Moffatt, he said, did not understand it. And as for Adam Clarke who spent 40 years writing his great commentary on the Bible—DJH says he did not understand God's plan! Don Waterhouse downgraded my late friend, Henry H. Halley, a saint who had memorized much of the Bible and who gave to the world his great Halley's *Bible Handbook.*

Do not establish a doctrine by a difficult verse, says DJH wisely, but he and other Armstrongites do that confusingly and repeatedly.

DJH refers to Acts 10:15, "What God hath cleansed, that call not thou common." He dodges this verse by saying Peter was perplexed (17) and then in verse 28, the application was to people—"I should not call any man common or unclean." But the passage *also* means that we may now eat pork, if we wish. Yet Armstrong legislates against it. Having lived on a farm in my youth, I know that chickens are no cleaner than pigs as to their diet. A minor matter.

I Timothy 4:1–5 speaks of those who forbid certain foods as those who have departed from the faith. ". . . commanding to abstain from foods, which God hath created to be received with thanksgiving by them who believe and know the truth. For every creature of God is good, and nothing to be refused, if it is received with thanksgiving. For it is sanctified by the Word of God and prayer."

Next, we must become fruit inspectors!

24

BY THEIR FRUITS
YE SHALL KNOW THEM

"WHEREFORE, BY THEIR fruits ye shall know them" (Matt. 7:20).

What IS the fruit of Armstrongism? It seems to be quite the opposite from the fruits of evangelical churches. For instance—

In 1970 the Southern Baptists gave over $50,000,000 to help *other* lands. These gifts supported 2501 missionaries, 234 kindergartens, 311 elementary schools, 82 secondary schools, 24 colleges, 51 seminaries, 124 hospitals and clinics, 21 orphan homes, and 41 good will centers—all in foreign countries. They have their 13,113 churches and missions in 76 nations, with 687,000 members and 60,000 baptisms in 1970. And this is only one denomination. Some others do still more good work proportionately.

In contrast, Armstrong gets and spends about $55,000,000 annually for propaganda to *hinder* such good churches. Jesus said, "Woe unto you . . . For ye have taken away the key of knowledge; ye entered not in yourselves, and them that were entering ye *hindered*" (Luke 11:52).

Armstrong "steals" the good seed of the Word of God which Christ and evangelical Christians plant (Luke 8:11, 12). Many people are "wayside hearers," easy prey to the cults which, like the devil, "taketh the Word out of their hearts, lest they should believe and be saved."

"But the fruit of the Spirit is love, joy, peace, long suffering, gentleness, goodness, faith, meekness, self control; against such there is no law" (Gal. 5:22, 23).

"But if ye be led by the Spirit, ye are not under the law" (Gal. 5:18).

Is Armstrong (HWA) led by the Spirit or by Jewish laws? For Armstrongites the Spirit *is dead;* they have killed His Personhood; they deny His Personality; they reduce Him to a mere force, an influence, an "it." They share the blasphemy of those who said, "God is Dead"—an awful insult. They borrowed this insult against the Holy Spirit from the so-called Jehovah's Witnesses. Since it is the Holy Spirit who is to guide us into "all truth" (John 16:13, where the *personal* pronoun is used for the Holy Spirit seven times), then Armstrongites are left without a guide.

With their Holy Spirit as a dead *thing,* no wonder HWA attacks the *body* of Christ which is His church. Christ's churches are *doing what He did*—teaching, preaching, healing, feeding, clothing, loving, nursing, comforting, warning, praying, fellowshiping. But HWA, like the devil (Rev. 12:10), accuses and attacks us constantly, worldwide.

1. *Is LOVE a fruit of Armstrongism?* Hardly. One test is 1 John 3:14, "We know that we have passed from death unto life, *because we love the brethren.* He that loveth not his brother abideth in death." But HWA says we are Satan's people; he calls us hateful names. This is not love!

Even so, the wicked Pharisees accused Christ of working for the devil (Matt. 12:24–30). They did this *after* He had healed a blind man. Did the Pharisees ever heal the blind? Has Armstrong ever built any hosptials or dispensaries or clinics anywhere? What GOOD has he done?

Christ answered His pharisaical accusers, "A house divided against itself cannot stand" (Matt. 12:25). "How can Satan cast out Satan?" (Mark 3:23). "He that is not with me is against me; and he that gathereth not with me scattereth" (Luke 11:23).

The Apostle Paul loved intensely, and he prayed intensely, that Israelites might be *saved* (Rom. 9:1–3; 10:1). Evangelical Christians do the same. But do HWA and his *ever* pray to get sinners saved? Contrary to Paul, HWA wants to announce a future kingdom—and gather proselytes.

Is love a fruit of Armstrongism? Not much. (Of course HWA will deny the facts we cite, but let him show real Christian fruits for a change.)

2. *Is JOY a fruit of Armstrongism?* Doubtful. They barter resurrection joys of Sundays for tomb-gloom Saturdays. They kill Christmas cheer and Easter rejoicing by elevating heathen gods. They boycott birthday pleasures on trumped-up excuses. They cannot, or will not, join the angels in rejoicing over each sinner saved (Luke 15:10). They do not rejoice with us in our revivals where sinners are genuinely saved for all eternity. They lose the great values in our many devotional and exegetical books, our beautiful hymns, and in sermons of Spirit-filled, Christ-honoring, faithful servants of God.

What joy is left for HWA's people who "separate themselves . . . have not the Spirit" (Jude 19)? According to their writings, they have joy in proselyting, in subtracting people from soul-winning churches, and in attacking all churches but their own.

What joy is there in observing Jewish sabbaths and feasts which were only shadows of Christian realities? What joy in sabbaths which were *never* commanded to Gentiles; yet this is their main foundation. What joy in needless abnegation, useless asceticism, and loveless Pharisaism?

An Armstrongite wrote to a friend, "Regarding the Holy Spirit, one can determine it (?) by its fruit." Notice the lifeless "it" for the Spirit. How can one find any joy in a dead Spirit?

3. *Is PEACE a fruit of Armstrongism?* Not much, if any. What peace was there for Ishmael "whose hand was *against* every man (Gen. 16:12)?

With no assurance of salvation in this life—contrary to many precious New Testament verses—how can HWA's people know peace? They may say they have peace, but their many un-Christian doctrines make it impossible.

With self-imposed bondage to old Jewish laws and rules and feasts, how do they know if they observe *all* of them? Do they remember these— "Eye for eye, tooth for tooth, hand for hand, foot for foot" (Exo. 21:24). "Offer the first of thy ripe fruits" (Exo. 22:29). Honest, now! "Make no mention of the names of other gods" (Exo. 23:13). They do. "Thou shalt not wear a garment of different sorts" (Deut. 22:11). "Make thee fringes upon the four quarters of thy vesture" (Deut. 22:12). "The woman shall not wear that which pertaineth to a man" (Deut. 22:5). "The man (sabbath breaker) shall surely be put to death" (Exo. 31:14). "Whosoever doeth ANY work in the sabbath day, he shall surely be put to death" (Exo. 31:15).

More. Cancel all loans every seventh year (Deut. 15:1-3). All land is to rest every seventh year (Lev. 25:1-7). Sliding scale of prices in view of the year of Jubilee (every fiftieth year) (Lev. 25:8-17).

What Christian, Gentile, or Jew can have peace with old Jewish laws now?

4. *Is LONG SUFFERING (patience) a fruit of Armstrongism?* Their bitter name-calling, denunciations, and condemnation are definite signs of anger, bad temper, and impatience. How can *any* accusation be worse than calling millions of real Christians the servants of Satan? And if, in self defense, someone answers these accusers, he is then called a persecutor. But at long last we must defend ourselves.

5. *Is GENTLENESS a fruit of Armstrongism?* Not according to the way they treat the body of Christ, His faithful and true churches. Of course no church is perfect; none was in New Testament times either, but Christ had gentleness and patience with each one.

The church is Christ's body. He loves it and gave Himself for it. He is as sensitive about attacks, wounds, assaults, bruises, and blows aimed at His body as any sane person is. Why not?

No, we are not perfect. But do all Armstrongites have halos; are they all saintly; is any one of them perfect?

6. *Is GOODNESS a fruit of Armstrongism?* No! HWA's boasted millions of listeners and readers are being propagandized into distrusting our good churches which have been *doing good works* ever since Christ built His first church. What is good about attacking good workers?

Our churches, with auxiliaries, have taught the illiterate, brought Bibles and good books to hundreds of tribes, sent the saving gospel of Christ to lost millions, healing to people with agonizing diseases; hospitals, doctors, nurses, and medicines. We have provided musical instruments, song books, paintings, and Christian literature. All this is GOODNESS; and it is fought by the Armstrong empire.

"For goodness' sake" add the Gideons, Youth for Christ, Campus Crusade, Inter-Varsity Christian Fellowship, Red Cross, Salvation Army, Rescue Missions, world relief, children's homes, retirement homes, and countless other good works. All this goodness is the result of our churches' influence.

What goodness has Armstrong done?

7. *Is FAITH (faithfulness) a fruit of Armstrongism?* Faith in HWA's propaganda, yes. Faith in the New Testament, not much.

Armstrongites are drawn mostly from backsliding and defecting members of true New Testament churches. They are proselytes. As such, they have proved *unfaithful* to their own churches. With self-imposed grievances from real or imaginary slights, they harbor resentments which grow with each telling. Their former pastors are favorite targets, for to oppose them indicates superiority over them. Then the martyr complex begins!

8. *Is MEEKNESS a fruit of Armstrongism?* Meekness is a willingness to learn from those who know, a respect for proper authority, and a good blend of humility with courtesy. Meekness is not weakness.

But HWA's followers reject authority from Christ's very best servants. They accept blandishments from strangers but not counsel from good pastors.

A little learning can be a dangerous thing; it can destroy meekness and good sense. Armed with a few of Armstrong's pamphlets, his followers will challenge the world's greatest scholars. Ignorant of church history, they believe HWA's teachings are new and fresh out of heaven! They know nothing of the 19 centuries of other heresies, dissensions, secessions, and "reform" movements of self-appointed saviors of the world. With minds wide open to believe the latest wind of doctrine, vacillating as a weather vane, they close their heads and hearts tightly against the time-tested, Spirit-filled, fruitful doctrines of saintly scholars of all denominations. Mr. Armstrong is not a meek man.

9. *Is TEMPERANCE (self control) a fruit of Armstrongism?* Those who are carried about by every wind of doctrine, by the sleight of men, and cunning craftiness" (Eph. 4:14)—such people lack self control. They show little or no temperance in accusing "the brethren."

These are the "wandering stars" of Jude 13; literally, planets without apparent order; such people will orbit around the latest persuasive speaker regardless of his disloyalty to New Testament doctrines.

We are told to "test the spirits whether they are of God; because many false prophets are gone out into the world" (1 John 4:1). We have tested Armstrongism and its alleged fruits. HWA has failed all nine of our tests.

Since HWA denies that the Holy Spirit is a Person, this alone puts him under much suspicion. Why should anyone want to downgrade the gentle, loving, comforting Holy Spirit? We are told not to grieve Him (Eph. 4:30). How can one grieve an "it"?

Surely the "God-is-dead" people grieve the Holy Spirit. So would the "Spirit-is-dead" people; such would "quench" Him effectively (1 Thes. 5:19).

Jesus said in Matthew 12:32, "whosoever speaketh *against* the Holy Spirit, it shall not be forgiven him. . ."

We want to speak up *for* the Holy Spirit. This will be our delightful task, next. For we do love Him, even as we love the Father and the Son. Let us pray that all Armstrongites, present and prospective, will receive *what the Bible says* about the blessed Holy Spirit.

We feel that the Holy Spirit wants us to love all Armstrongites, but not their doctrines.

25

THE HOLY SPIRIT
IS A PERSON

> Nevertheless, when HE, the Spirit of truth, is come, HE will guide you into all truth; for HE shall not speak of HIMSELF, but whatever HE shall hear, that shall HE speak; and HE will show you things to come.
> HE shall glorify me; for HE shall receive of mine, and shall show it unto you (John 16:13, 14).

"WHOSOEVER SPEAKETH AGAINST the Holy Spirit, it shall not be forgiven him, neither in this age, neither in the age to come" (Matt. 12:31). This solemn warning, first spoken by Christ to evil Pharisees (Matt. 12:24-30), seems to fit Armstrongism.

It is true that the King James Version has "itself" in Romans 8:16, 26 for the Holy Spirit. The RSV corrects this error. Greek grammar allows the neuter for persons on occasion, but not English. Dr. A. T. Robertson: It is a grave mistake to use the neuter "it" or "itself" when referring to the Holy Spirit *(Word Pictures in the New Testament,* IV, 374).

Mr. Armstrong (HWA) says the Holy Spirit is not a Person, but a Spirit. But God is also a Spirit (John 4:24), and we do not deny His Personality. HWA is determined to attack the Trinity, calling it a pagan concept. In this he follows the Jehovah's Witnesses. But Christ referred to the Holy Spirit repeatedly as "He" and Christ never borrowed pagan concepts.

Anyone following Armstrongism disqualifies himself from 1 John 4:1, "Beloved, believe not every spirit, but test the spirits whether they are of God; because many false prophets are gone out into the world." By downgrading the Holy Spirit from a Person to an "it," one loses all ability to test false cults as to their many heresies.

Let us see exactly what the Bible says.

I. *The Holy Spirit Has Personality; He Is a Person.*

1. The Holy Spirit creates and gives life (Job 33:4).

2. He appoints and commissions ministers (Isa. 48:16; Acts 13:2; 20:28).

3. He directs ministers where to preach (Acts 8:29; 10:19, 20; 16:6, 7).

4. He spoke in and by the prophets (Acts 1:16; 1 Peter 1:11, 12; 2 Peter 1:21).

5. He strives with sinners (Gen. 6:3).

6. He reproves and guides (John 16:8, 13).

7. He comforts (Acts 9:31) and helps our infirmities (Rom. 8:26).

8. He teaches (John 14:26; 1 Cor. 12:3).

9. He sanctifies (Rom. 15:16; 1 Cor. 6:11).

10. He testifies of Christ and glorifies Him (John 15:26; 16:14).

11. He has a power of His own (Rom. 15:13.

12. He searches all things (Rom. 11:33, 34 with 1 Cor. 2:10, 11).

13. He works according to His will (1 Cor. 12:11).

14. He dwells with real Christians (John 14:17).

15. He can be grieved (Eph. 4:30); vexed (Isa. 63:10); resisted (Acts 7:51) and tempted (Acts 5:9).

More: since we are "born of the Spirit," HWA invalidates our means of salvation (John 3:5). He weakens or cancels the inspiration of the Bible (1 Cor. 2:13; 2 Peter 1:21). HWA also wrecks the administrative work of the Holy Spirit for our churches by denying His personality.

II. *The Holy Spirit Is God.*

1. He is called God (Acts 5:3, 4).

2. He is joined with the Father and the Son (Matt. 28:19).

3. He is eternal (Heb. 9:14).

4. He is omnipresent (Psalm 139:7-14).

5. He is omniscient (1 Cor. 2:10).

6. He is omnipotent (Luke 1:35; Rom. 15:19).

7. He is creator (Gen. 1:2, 26, 27 with Job 33:4).

8. He is equal to and one with Father and Son (2 Cor. 13:14).

9. He raised Christ from the dead (Acts 2:24; 1 Peter 3:18; Heb. 13:20; Rom. 1:4).

10. He is source of wisdom (1 Cor. 12:8; Isa. 11:2; John 16:13).

11. He is source of miraculous power (Matt. 12:28 with Luke 11:20).

12. He is Comforter for all Christians (Acts 9:31 with 2 Cor. 1:3).

13. He sanctifies real Christians (Rom. 15:16).

Surely the Holy Spirit has His place in the Holy Trinity!

III. *The Holy Spirit Is Our Comforter.*

1. He communicates joy to Christians (Rom. 14:17; Gal. 5:22; 1 Th. 1:6).

2. He edifies our churches (Acts 9:31).

3. He testifies to and reminds us of Christ our Savior (John 15:26).

4. He imparts the love of God to us (Rom. 5:3-5).

5. He imparts hope to us (Rom. 15:13; Gal. 5:5).

6. He dwells in us and teaches us (John 14:17, 26).

7. He abides forever with each believer (John 14:16).

8. He is sent to us by Christ, from the Father; therefore He is a distinct Personality (John 14:25; 15:26).

Thank God for the Holy Spirit! How wonderful is His ministry to us! Let us pray that all who doubt or deny Him will soon repent, and then enjoy His tender loving care.

IV. *The Holy Spirit Is Our Teacher.*

1. He reveals the things of God to us (1 Cor. 2:10, 13).

2. He reveals the things of Christ to us (John 16:14).

3. He reveals the future (Luke 2:26; Acts 21:11).

4. He reminds us of the words of Christ (John 14:26).

5. He directs us in the way of godliness (Isa. 30:21; Ezek. 36:27).

6. He teaches us how to answer persecutors (Mark 13:11; Luke 12:12).

7. He enables ministers to teach (1 Cor. 12:8).

8. He guides us into all truth (John 14:26; 16:13).

9. He directs decisions of good churches (Acts 15:28).

10. We must heed His instructions (Rev. 2:7, 11, 29; 1 Cor. 2:9, 10).

11. He is given in answer to prayer (Luke 11:13; Eph. 1:16, 17).

12. Unbelievers do not receive Him (1 Cor. 2:14).

(Personally, I feel rebuked when reading all these precious promises, for I have too often failed to receive what the Spirit wants to give us.)

V. *The Holy Spirit Is IN the Trinity.*

1. He is eternal (Rom. 16:26 with Rev. 22:13; Heb. 9:14).

2. He is holy (Rev. 4:8; 15:4 with Acts 3:14; 1 John 2:20).

3. He is true (John 7:28 with Rev. 3:7).

4. He is omnipresent (Jer. 23:24 with Eph. 1:23; Psalm 139:7).

5. He is omnipotent (Gen. 17:1 with Rev. 1:8; Rom. 15:19; Jer. 32:17).

6. He is omniscient (Acts 15:18 with John 21:17; 1 Cor. 2:10, 11).

7. He is creator (Gen. 1:2; Col. 1:16; Job 33:4; John 1:3).

8. He heads spiritual work (1 Cor. 12:11; Col. 1:29; Heb. 13:21).

9. He is source of eternal life (Rom. 6:23 with John 10:28; Gal. 6:8).

10. He raised Christ from the dead 11 Cor. 6:14; John 2:19; 1 Peter 3:18).

11. He supplies ministers (Jer. 3:15; Eph. 4:11; Acts 13:2; 20:28).

12. He saves us (2 Thes. 2:13, 14; Titus 3:4-6; 1 Peter 1:2).

13. He is in our baptismal formula (Matt. 28:19).

14. He is in our benedictions (2 Cor. 13:14).

With all this evidence, how can anyone still deny the Trinity?

VI. *The Holy Spirit Is Distinct from His Gifts.*

"God anointed Jesus of Nazareth with the Holy Spirit, AND with power" in Acts 10:38.

Christ said of the Holy Spirit, "He shall glorify me; for he shall receive of mine, and shall show it unto you" (John 16:14).

The Holy Spirit prays for us. "The Spirit also helpeth our infirmities . . . the Spirit himself maketh intercession for us" (Rom. 8:26).

". . . abound in hope, through the power of the Holy Spirit" (Rom. 15:13).

The Holy Spirit has many gifts for us: wisdom, knowledge, faith, healing, miracles, prophecy, discerning of spirits—this latter helps us to identify and understand the heresies in cults. This "very same Spirit gives to every man severally as He will" (1 Cor. 12:4-11).

VII. *The Holy Spirit May Be Sinned Against.*

He can be resisted and vexed (Isa. 63:10), and outraged (Heb. 10:29).

He can be blasphemed and spoken against, or downgraded (Matt. 12:31).

He can be lied to, the same as to God (Acts 5:3, 4, 9).

He can be grieved. "And grieve not the Holy Spirit of God, by whom ye are sealed unto the day of redemption" (Eph. 4:30). Since He loves us (Rom. 15:30), we should receive His love to us, and reciprocate it. To be shunned by someone we love is to grieve us. This PERSON, The Holy Spirit, loves us. A "force" or an "influence" cannot do that!

The Holy Spirit is mentioned in every New Testament book except 2 and 3 John. He gives us access to the Father (Eph. 2:18). He frees us from Old Testament bondage (2 Cor. 3:17).

May the Holy Spirit lead us into all truth, and into the power of God.

26

HOW YOU CAN BE IMBUED WITH THE POWER OF GOD

MR. HERMAN L. HOEH wrote a tract with the above title. I wrote to him, months ago, requesting a reply, but none has come. My letter—

Mr. Hoeh, you say that our churches are insipid and inane and without spiritual zeal, etc. Some are, but a *great many* churches are filled with soul-winning power, real spiritual power. See the book by Towns, *The Ten Largest Sunday Schools.* Over 400 responded to the gospel in one day, in one church. And many evangelists have great spiritual power.

You say that the churches do not look to the right source of power, but many do! We have *more* powerful, fruitful, Biblical, effective, and happy churches now than ever before.

You imply that non-Armstrongites have their "thoughts corrupted" but what cult has more actual errors per page than Armstrongism? You insist on using "it" for the Holy Spirit. Isn't this corrupting the doctrine of the blessed Holy Spirit who has all the attributes of personality?

You insist on us keeping the Ten Commandments, but the Book of Romans shows that the old Jewish laws are now dead (Rom. 7:6); that Christians are now "become dead to the law by the body of Christ" (7:4); that we are now delivered from the law (7:6); and that we are not under the law, but under grace (Rom. 6:14, 15; Gal. 5:18).

You refer to the Holy Spirit as the "germ" of eternal life! No such phrase or concept is found in the Bible.

147

So no one can be born of God until the resurrection? But 1 John 3:2 says, "Beloved, NOW are we the sons of God." This glorious truth has been believed and enjoyed by millions of genuine born-again Christians.

You say that to be filled with the Spirit (Eph. 5:18) does not mean emotional manifestations, but the Bible says otherwise. Galatians 5:22, 23 lists several good emotions as evidence of the Spirit's indwelling. Love, joy, and peace are splendid spiritual emotions, given by the Holy Spirit.

So no one in the Old Testament prayed to the Father? See Psalm 5:1-3; 65:2; 89:26; 99:6; Isaiah 9:6; 63:16; 64:8.

And you tell us that God "is a family," but the Bible never says that. And the Council of Nicea did not invent the Trinity truth. This was always accepted, except for heretics like the Arians. The Trinity is not from the pagan Babylonians; it IS in the Bible.

Even though 1 John 5:7 is not in some of the ancient manuscripts, we have plenty of proof for the Trinity nevertheless. And as for your accusing unnamed persons of "a deliberate hoax," how do you prove it? Matthew 28:19 DOES refer to the Trinity in unmistakable terms. How could it be any plainer? Each of the three precious Names is on a par with each other, or equality; all are deity; each one is a Personality.

The Holy Spirit has Personality. He is classed with other Persons. The Holy Spirit acts as only a Person can act. "Grieve not the Holy Spirit of God" (Eph. 4:30).

Your comments, please. (No answer after many months of waiting. If one "plays dumb" when writing, a reply might come.)

＊　＊　＊

Later, I have often wondered if some verses in the Book of Jude might apply to the Armstrong writers. "These are they who separate themselves, sensual, having not the Spirit" (Jude 19). Consider—

1. Does the Holy Spirit lead *anyone* to separate himself from 99% of dedicated, intelligent, Spirit-filled, soul-winning, Bible-believing, humble, and honest Christian pastors and people?

2. Does the Holy Spirit lead anyone to trust strangers, however cunning in clever advertising, contrary to hundreds of real Christian friends?

3. Does the *Holy* Spirit lead anyone to join atheists, Jews, and

other Christ-rejecters in their disrespect for Sundays, Easters, and Christmases?

4. Would the Holy Spirit endorse a self-appointed "prophet" who is brash enough to boast that he alone in all the world of Christians is right, and was chosen to give the *only* true gospel as of January 7, 1934? In all the Bible, did God *ever* approve such arrogance and bigotry?

5. Does the Holy Spirit endorse Armstrong any more than many other self-appointed prophets as Joe Smith, Mrs. E. G. White, Mrs. Eddy, Charles Russell, Mrs. Annie Besant, Father Divine, etc.?

6. Does the Holy Spirit lead anyone to ignore or deny the scores of New Testament verses that free us from Jewish legalism? But Armstrong misreads a few verses; he wants to bind his people to Jewish laws, salvation-kept-by-works, self righteousness, and presumed superiority.

7. Will the Holy Spirit, like HWA, downgrade *millions* of honest, fair, courteous, Bible-loving, devout, just, prayerful, gracious, neighborly, and intelligent members of our churches— all downgraded in order to puff up the self-righteous Armstrongites? Not likely!

Sorry to be so negative—but MUCH of the Bible is negative, and repetitive. Persistent dangers call for continued warnings.

27

WHAT DO YOU MEAN....
KINGDOM OF GOD?

WHAT WORD, OR words, ought we to use for a màn who says that no one has been right on Christian truth during the past 1,864 years except himself? Yet that is just what H. W. Armstrong (HWA) says about himself, again.

In his tract on the above title, HWA insists that the world did not know the profound truths which came only to himself, and that churches have not preached it for 18½ centuries. Then, suddenly, God called HWA, a self-confessed failure in three ventures, to tell the whole world HIS exact "plain truth." He repeats this claim, endlessly. Analyzing him—

1. HWA implies that the Kingdom of God was first preached by Christ (Matt. 4:17), but John the Baptist preached it first (Matt. 3:2).

2. HWA says the apostles were sent to preach "only" the Kingdom of God, but he errs again. They preached to get a great many people converted, and then baptized those converts (John 4:1, 2).

3. HWA feigns surprise that the world is ignorant of what he alone discovered (?) in 1934. This is another of his psychological pranks which is intended to make readers trust his superior (!) knowledge.

4. Then because not one Christian in 1,864 years knew what HWA then knew, he says a counterfeit gospel had to be invented (before that of HWA!).

5. He seems very sure that Daniel 7 with Revelation 13 and 17 refer to the Common Market countries of Europe in this present generation.

6. He says that the only four worldwide empires that ever existed were prophesied in Daniel. What about the British Empire whose boast for many years was, "The sun never sets on the British Empire."

7. HWA implies again that no one will enter the kingdom of heaven until the resurrection. But Colossians 1:13 says that God "hath delivered us from the power of darkness, and *hath translated us* into the kingdom of His dear Son." We enter the spiritual kingdom at our conversion, and into the physical kingdom later (John 3:3, 5; Col. 4:11; Rev. 1:9).

8. HWA says Abraham is not yet in the kingdom, citing as his proof texts Hebrews 11:13, 39, 40 but these verses do not even mention the kingdom.

9. HWA misleads the unwary by assuming that every mention of "kingdom" means an earthly one. Not so, for Christ's present kingdom is spiritual, although He will be actual King of an earthly kingdom later.

10. HWA says again that Judah seceded from Israel, but the Bible says the exact opposite (1 Kings 12:16-24).

11. For naive readers, HWA adroitly connects the ten tribes with the ten servants in Luke 19:11-27). (Why not the ten virgins, or ten lepers?) Here he mixes iron and clay, oil and water, fact and fiction. He tries to weld them together but his gaps are showing and his joints are bad. A bridge with such poor workmanship would fall. Perhaps we need another chapter on humor. Like—"a butcher backed into his meat grinder and got a little behind in his work" (*Chicago Tribune*)!

12. Lacking facts, HWA resorts to emotion in order to win followers. He labels us who distrust him as paganized, empty, deceived, false prophets—all to make himself and his credulous adherents feel superior.

But the Bible says the kingdom of God includes all believers since John the Baptist first won real converts (Matt. 3:2; Luke 16:16). For only such converts obey the *kingly* rule of Christ, so that the kingdom is now *within* them. The kingdom is not synonymous with the church, but all converted church members are in the kingdom.

The first task of churches is to get individuals soundly converted—and thus into the kingdom of Christ now. Thus the churches are the "cutting edges" of the ever-growing kingdom. It will be so until Christ returns.

"The kingdom of heaven is likened unto a man who sowed good seed in his field; but, while men slept, *his enemy* came and sowed tares among the wheat, and went his way . . ." (Matt. 13).

Since Christ spoke those words, many enemies have come and gone, planting noxious weeds among the good grain of true Christians. One of the latest enemies, loudest, most universal, and with the worst assortment of weeds, is HWA. Whatever he discusses in the Bible, he distorts. To what good purpose? Who benefits? His many employees do financially, up to $40,000 in annual salary.

The Ambassador colleges are not the kingdom of God. Too many young people are lured there to become brain-washed by HWA's teachers; then they go out to attack Christ's churches which are His body. While they talk peace they continually make war on the pastors and churches who are doing Christ's will. "I am for peace; but when I speak, they are for war" (Psalm 120:7).

Mr. Armstrong attacks so very many New Testament doctrines, and so wildly, that he comes dangerously close to committing the unpardonable sin. We handle this terribly dangerous sin with extra care—next.

28

ARMSTRONG FLIRTS WITH THE UNPARDONABLE SIN

MR. HERBERT W. ARMSTRONG (HWA) wrote a tract on this awful sin. But when he "speaks against the Holy Spirit" (Matt. 12:32) as he has done, he is perilously close to committing the unpardonable sin himself. He begins his tract by saying that Acts 16:31 is not quite true, or enough true! "Believe on the Lord Jesus Christ, and thou shalt be saved, and thy house."

This verse IS true. It saved the Philippian jailer and his household, as it has saved many others. It contains the plan of salvation which is all of grace—not part law as HWA's garbled "gospel" has it. Analyzing—

To "believe" means *complete commitment*. It is much more than mental assent to an idea; it is full acceptance of Christ as Lord.

To believe on the "Lord" means to receive Him as Master, King, and complete Ruler of our lives. "Lord" means authority —full authority.

To believe in "Jesus" means to receive Him as Savior from all one's sins—past, present, and future. The name "Jesus" means Savior, and when we receive Him as such, He forgives ALL our sins.

To believe on "Christ" means to receive Him as God's Anointed One, sent to the world as the only begotten Son of God. He is God's agent. He fulfilled all Old Testament laws so that we do not need to, even as He died to pay our penalty for breaking those laws. He came to die for us, thus atoning for all our sins. He rose again, and He will come again.

Immediately upon believing we are saved. Salvation comes as soon as we commit our lives fully to Christ. The repentant thief received immediate salvation (Luke 23:43); so does every repentant soul.

This gracious promise is extended to every responsible member of one's household. Each person must believe and receive for himself. The New Testament has no room for proxy religion, nor for HWA's legalism. HWA tries to negate Acts 16:31, for it negates his legalistic system.

Acts 16:32, 33 tells how Paul and Silas taught the jailer's family more, and then baptized them. Thus Paul and Silas were sure each person was really saved, all apart from works or Old Testament laws.

Yet HWA puts salvation in the future tense. He *robs his own people* of the joys of present salvation. And he maligns the believers in John 7:31 by saying they were the same people as in John 8:31-46 who tried to kill Jesus. Awful! HWA also accuses present-day soul winners who pass out tracts as being the same kind of Christ-killers (p. 7 of his tract).

HWA does have some good comments on the Christian's two natures (Gal. 16, 17). If he would only apply the same good reasoning in his comments on 1 John 3:9, he would be more consistent than he is.

HWA accuses unjustly those Christians who believe that 2 Corinthians 3:11-14 supersedes the Ten Commandments, saying such people condone sin. We do NOT condone sin; we now have a higher and better law than the Old Testament had. We now live in NEW Testament times, not in the Old.

HWA also errs in saying that most passages on salvation refer to its taking place at Christ's coming. This is not true.

For 19 centuries plus, uncounted millions of people have been truly saved, have been prayerful, Spirit-led, fruitful, genuine Christians. Yet, suddenly HWA accuses us of being Satan's because we worship on Sundays. He attacks us even as Christ's foes attacked Him in Matthew 12:24-32.

Christ defined the unpardonable sin in Matthew 12:31, 32, ". . . the blasphemy against the Holy Spirit, it shall not be forgiven men . . . whosoever speaketh against the Holy Spirit, it shall not be forgiven him, neither in this age, neither in the age to come." Isn't HWA guilty of exactly that—speaking against the Holy Spirit, and speaking against Christians who are filled with the Holy Spirit? and in negating Spirit-inspired words such as Acts 16:31? HWA degrades the Holy Spirit from Personal deity to an impersonal force—an "it." How can such a lie-filled cult as Armstrongism survive except by the power of Satan?

Now HWA finally comes to his own definition of the unpardonable sin, one different from what Christ said it is. HWA has two points: deliberately choosing to live contrary to God's revealed will (meaning HWA's will!); or, by continual neglect of all Christian privileges and obligations. Of course HWA means by this, neglect of HWA's ministry and Old Testament Jewish laws. But he does issue a good warning about sinning wilfully (Heb. 10:26–29), a warning that Christian preachers have been giving for over 19 centuries.

If any reader is worried now about his having committed the unpardonable sin, such worry is evidence that the Holy Spirit is pleading with him and that he still may be saved. If you are such a person, please read and believe Acts 16:31, firmly, sincerely and thoroughly. Then you will be saved, NOW. You have God's Word for it. Isn't that enough?

Now for the extremely interesting subject of Predestination.

29

PREDESTINATION: THE BIBLE vs. ARMSTRONG

AN ANONYMOUS ARMSTRONG writer has a tract on Predestination. He boasts of knowledge superior to that of 99% of the world's Christians. He also accuses us of living in confusion and in "Babylon." And he tries desperately to gain merit or distinction by differing from other Bible readers who are as intelligent as he is, and far more discerning.

Predestination is briefly explained in 1 Peter 1:2, "Elect according to the foreknowledge of God, the Father, through sanctification of the Spirit, unto obedience and sprinkling of the blood of Jesus Christ."

The word "elect" means much the same as "predestination." Both are based on the foreknowledge of God. Being omniscient, God knows in advance what we will do under all circumstances, even with our free will with which every decision we make is our own. Thus predestination is merely stating what God knows about us beforehand.

By the way, 1 Peter 1:2 is a clear declaration of the Trinity, and of the value of the precious blood of Christ. Armstrong denies the first and minimizes the second, much to the loss of his followers.

And the Bible, contrary to Armstrongism, does tell of only two classes—saved and lost (Mark 16:16; Luke 19:10; John 5: 24-29).

And HWA (for Armstrongism) errs again in saying that God

is not trying to save sinners in this age. *But He is.* "Go . . . make disciples (converts)" (Matt. 28:19). "For the Son of man is come to seek and to *save* that which was lost" (Luke 19:10; also, John 3:16, 36; 20:31; Rom. 9:1–3; 10:1; Jude 23, etc.).

Repeatedly, HWA assumes that the Old Testament covered only 4000 years, but we know it was much longer. Many Old Testament chronologies are incomplete. The Jews understood that "father" could mean a grandfather, or one even still further removed. HWA must know this, but he "has an axe to grind." He *must* prove his pet theories.

HWA accuses God of blinding the majority of people so they will not receive the gospel. This is a terribly serious accusation. Why, then, did God send His Son to save sinners? No; people blind themselves by their continued sinning, just as Egypt's pharaoh hardened his own heart by continued stubbornness. It is the devil who blinds sinners (2 Cor. 4:4).

And again HWA makes English-speaking people to be Israelites—a term interchangeable with "Jews." But those who say they are Jews, and are not, are liars and are under a curse (Rev. 2:9; 3:9).

The millennium of Revelation 20 is not called a "Sabbath," but HWA builds doctrines on such false assumptions and mis-representations.

HWA repeats, by strong inference, that only he and his followers really understand the plan of salvation, or the future in prophecy. But isn't it true that most cult leaders have similar egotism? It seems to be a mark of false prophets.

This tract errs again in saying, or implying, that predestination is found only four times in the Bible. Here he conveniently omits knowledge of the Greek New Testament; for *proorizo,* the word for predestination is found two more places—in Acts 4:28 and in 1 Corinthians 2:7.

And since predestination has to do with our salvation (contrary to HWA), then by inference it means lack of salvation for others. Perhaps HWA's writers should do better homework.

But they write on and on. And we can answer them fully on every point of difference with evangelical Christians, for we have read the Bible 60 years. In addition, we have access to the accumulated wisdom of centuries of Bible scholarship which exposes heresies as well as it expounds the sacred Scriptures.

The Book of Titus has a relevant passage here. "Holding fast the faithful word as he hath been taught, that he may be able by sound doctrine both to exhort and to confute the opposers.

"For there are many unruly and vain talkers and decievers, specially they of the circumcision (legalizers, like Armstrong),

"*Whose mouths must be stopped,* who subvert whole houses, teaching things which they ought not, for filthy lucre's sake" (Titus 1:9-11). "Lucre" here is *kerdos*, meaning gain, profit or advantage. Just how "filthy" HWA's reputed income of 55 millions in 1972 would be is not for us to judge; the Lord will handle that matter. In the meantime, we are told to use "sound doctrine" to "confute the opposers" and stop the mouths of "vain talkers and deceivers."

Now, what about immortality? It deserves careful attention.

30

IF YOU DIE,
WILL YOU LIVE AGAIN?

Mr. C. Paul Meredith (CPM) writes an Armstrongite tract on Immortality. According to pattern, he begins with a slur on all preachers but his own. The preachers, CPM says, are all unaware of the fact (?) that the entire Bible is concerned with only one subject, the *future* kingdom of God. And this kingdom will not begin until the resurrection, he says.

If by "kingdom" he means salvation through Christ who NOW brings us into the present heavenly kingdom, well and good. But he is not concerned about salvation *now*. He is far more anxious for us to leave our good churches and become paying members of Armstrong's empire.

CPM says we cannot be born again until the resurrection. But the Bible contradicts him repeatedly, as we have already shown. See Ephesians 2:8.

CPM repeats the error that Christ died on a Wednesday and rose on Saturday (which would then be the fourth day). Great scholars like Dr. A. T. Robertson are better experts in Greek than Armstrongites.

CPM denies that we are born with immortal souls, and offers as proof 1 Corinthians 15:47, "The first man is of the earth, earthy." Such "proof" is as weak as most of his arguments. Our next chapter deals with the status of souls between death and resurrection.

Then CPM quotes backslidden Solomon (Eccl. 3:19, 20) in

his attempt to show that man dies like animals die. But Solomon was reasoning "under the sun," apart from God. This explains his erratic, mistaken, materialistic ideas—upon which some cults now love to feed.

And because Acts 2:29 refers to David's *body* now being in the grave, CPM tries to tell us that man dies like a dog. See our next chapter. In reference to the Holy Spirit (p. 3), CPM uses "it." This is not being fair or courteous to the Third Person of the Deity.

CPM says that God is not trying to save many people *now*. But how could God do more to save people than He is now doing? And are not all Armstrongites trying to hinder our churches from winning more souls? Where would the Armstrong devotees be now if our churches had not kept the gospel alive and progressing throughout *previous* generation?

CPM tries to accommodate the unsaved dead by adding a resurrection or two hereafter in order to give them an alleged "first chance" to be saved. He is holding out false hopes, on utterly false bases.

Still more fantastic is CPM's assertion that only Christ has been born into God's kingdom thus far, and not even Christ until His resurrection! He offers as "proof" texts Romans 8:29 and Colossians 1:18, but these verses are no proof at all. *Of course,* Christ is first; He is first in God's kingdom for all eternity, first in resurrection, and first in our affection. He was *always* first. He did not suddenly become so on that wonderful Easter morning.

And CPM implies that when Christ rose from the dead that only *then* was He raised to immortality. As though He was not immortal before that! Even HWA calls Him, in his many Old Testament references, "The Eternal"— meaning Christ in His Old Testament character.

But HWA wants to differ in as many points as possible from most of the intelligent, fruitful, Spirit-filled Christians. Thus Armstrongism is meant to stand out as superior, in *their* estimation. It is like the tone-deaf choir singer who doesn't know he is off key!

A great longing overwhelms me again. It is that all Armstrong's propagandists would seriously examine the bases of their own salvation. Are they sure of salvation? If not, receive

Christ into your hearts now, by faith. Trust and obey, For there's no other way. To be happy in Jesus, But to trust and obey.

Consider Saul of Tarsus who, like Armstrong, persecuted the churches. "I verily thought within myself, that I ought to do many things contrary to the name of Jesus of Nazareth, Which thing I also did . . . I gave my voice against them (Christians) . . . And I punished them often in every synagogue . . . even unto foreign cities" (Acts 26:9–11).

Then Saul of Tarsus got soundly converted and became Paul the Apostle. He began winning souls to Christ, planting new churches, bearing persecution, and writing his inspired epistles. He then used his superb education and his many skills FOR the churches instead of AGAINST them.

Pray God that the Armstrong people will soon do likewise. Think what good they could do with their present equipment!

❋ ❋ ❋

Our next question is, Will you die as a beast dies? Or, will you die as the repentant thief, the martyr Stephen, and the apostle Paul—each of whom were sure of heavenly bliss right after death?

31

ARE SOULS CONSCIOUS BETWEEN DEATH AND RESURRECTION?

THIS CHAPTER WILL serve to answer an article by Garner Ted Armstrong entitled, "Do You Have an Immortal Soul?"

Are souls conscious between death and resurrection? For answers to this great question we rely on the Bible. No other book has authority in this field. Of what help are Bultman or Moltman, Barth or Brunner, Niebuhr or Tillich? Their value lies chiefly in stimulating Hegelian dialectic, in suggesting liberalism or agnosticism, and occasionally in their off-beat references to our Holy Bible.

1. *Our Lord Jesus Taught Soul Consciousness after Death.*

When Jesus contended with the unbelievers in His day, He left us much food for thought. And He had many arguments with them. In the Fourth Gospel alone may be found 18 such encounters. Then we need not fear any confrontation with unbelievers if we are prepared.

The Sadducees in New Testament times were no mean adversaries. They prided themselves on their superior knowledge. No doubt they called themselves intellectuals, or intelligentsia, in contrast to ordinary Pharisees who believed in angels and in a future resurrection.

In Matthew 22:23-33, the Sadducees *thought* they had a foolproof case to use against Christ and against soul-consciousness after death. But Jesus referred them to Exodus 3 where God appeared to Moses in the bush and said, "I am the God of thy father, the God of Abraham, the God of Isaac, and the God of Jacob." Jesus quoted this verse and then added the clincher, "God is not the God of the dead, but of the living" (Matt. 22: 32). This was spoken *before* the resurrection, during the time *between* the patriarchs' deaths and resurrection, and it declares that Abraham, Isaac, and Jacob were then living but without their physical bodies.

This argument by Christ is repeated in Mark 12:26, 27 and Luke 20:37, 38, indicating its great importance. Luke adds the significant phrase, "For all live unto him." These three passages tell us that not only was God the God of Abraham, Isaac and Jacob during their earthly life times—for this would have been no answer at all to the Sadducees—but that He is their God NOW. Their immortal souls live with Him forever.

Admittedly, this passage deals primarily with the future resurrection, but it is also proof of the present existence of departed souls. For if these patriarchs had ceased to *exist*, then they would need much more than a resurrection. They would need a new creation, for how can there be a resurrection of that which no longer exists?

2. *The Story of the Rich Man and Lazarus Indicates Immortality.*

This passage in Luke 16:19–31 is not properly a parable; it is rather an account of an actual happening. Parables do not usually name any historic character whereas this story names two, and the third is anonymous for the sake of courtesy. And this incident took place long before the resurrection. The beggar died and was carried away by the angels into Abraham's bosom. "The rich man died also, and was buried, and in Hades he lifted up his eyes, being in torments, and seeth Abraham afar off, and Lazarus in his bosom" (Luke 16:22, 23). The rich man could see, suffer, speak, recognize a neglected beggar, and he could pray—all at the same time that his five brothers were physically alive. How urgent, then, should be our evangelism in order to win souls now.

3. *The Repentant Thief on the Cross Tells Us of the Future.*

This one thief had joined the other, at first, in reviling Christ on the cross. But he repented. This was amazing; for he looked on the bloody, bruised, and impaled body of Christ, crowned with thorns, reviled by soldiers and priests alike—and saw in

Him a King! What remarkable faith he had! We have a hard time getting people now to believe in a clean, comforting, and conquering Christ. We sit in comfortable pews, with everyone in Sunday-best clothing and with smiles and handshakes, lovely music and trained speakers—and yet many still refuse to repent. But this thief, in great physical agony, showed real remorse and genuine conversion. His prayer was quickly answered, for Christ responded: "Verily I say unto you, Today shalt thou be with me in Paradise" (Luke 23:43).

Here is future retention of identity and continuing companionship for both Christ and the saved person. And this would not be in a grave which they did not share, but in paradise-heaven.

Now we know from John's Gospel that both Christ and the thief died that day, before sunset (John 19:31–33). And they were both in paradise that very day. Those who cavil about the comma being after the word "Today" forget that these two had likely never met before that day, and they would not meet on earth after that day. And where in all literature is ever found such an awkward expression as "I say to you today?"

And as to paradise being named, and not heaven, "Where Jesus is, 'Tis heaven there." It is a great comfort to believe Christ here instead of modern Sadducees who try their best to contradict Him.

4. *Certain Old Testament Passages Seem to Indicate Total Death.*

Psalm 6:5 is a part of David's prayer. "For in death there is no remembrance of Thee; in Sheol who shall give Thee thanks?" This is spoken from the viewpoint of earthbound creatures. We are not able to communicate with the dead, and the dead are not able to speak to us. Phenomenally, this verse makes sense, but further revelation indicates that God has made us for more than earthly physical living. The grave, or Sheol, is not the end; it is rather a transfer point. Even though the natural man cannot understand existence after bodily death, he that is spiritual accepts God's Word and believes that our Creator has made us for greater things than this earth knows.

Ecclesiastes 3:19 has a strange sound. "For that which befalleth the sons of men befalleth beasts; even one thing befalleth them: as the one dieth, so dieth the other; yea, they have all one breath; and man hath no preeminence above the beasts:

for all is vanity." Now we know that animals and man share much of life and death in common, but we also believe that man *does* have preeminence above beasts. Solomon was writing as a backslider, "under the sun," with God left out. He is typical of modern materialists who ignore their Creator. Like too many evolutionists, they try frantically to find anything on earth, and now on the moon, to support their contention, and to support atheism. They are poor company for Christians who believe in God's higher plan for His own.

Ecclesiastes 9:5 and 10 are also records of uninspired writing. "The dead know not anything, neither have they any more a reward; for the memory of them is forgotten . . . for there is no work, nor device, nor knowledge, nor wisdom in Sheol, whither thou goest." Limiting oneself to an animal's viewpoint, "under the sun," these verses make sense. But a Christian has a higher dimension, a higher viewpoint, and a greater future after death than animals have.

Isaiah 38:18 records Hezekiah's thoughts after his prayer for healing had been assured. He wanted to live longer, knowing that only while he lived could he praise God and witness for Him. Verse 18 shows this, "For Sheol cannot praise Thee, death cannot celebrate Thee; They that go down into the pit cannot hope for Thy truth." We read here what one man *thought,* but we have no guarantee that all his thoughts were divinely inspired or correct.

The American Standard Version "Sheol" is often used for the "grave" of the King James Version; it means the end of human activity on earth as it appears to us *now.* Like the New Testament use of the word "sleep" for death, it can be misleading. But in John 11:11–14 Jesus clearly equates the sleep of Lazarus with physical death; so does Luke in Acts 7:60 with Stephen, and Paul in 1 Corinthians 11:30 for those judged in connection with taking the Lord's Supper in an unworthy manner.

   5. *Other Old Testament Passages Teach Soul Consciousness after Death.*

In Genesis 25:8 we read that when Abraham died he was "gathered to his people." But his father was buried in Haran and his grandparents likely in Ur of Chaldea. The meaning must be that Abraham's soul was united with those of his ancestors, right after death.

Genesis 35:29 says that when Isaac died he "was gathered unto his people." Genesis 49:33 says that when Jacob died, and before his burial, that he "was gathered unto his people." See also Judges 2:10; Deut. 32:50.

Exodus 3:6, 13 tell us that God is the God of Abraham, Isaac, and Jacob who had all died long before. More, the Lord told Moses, "this is my name forever, and this is my memorial unto all generations." So all people of Israel were to believe in this God of their departed fathers. Their God would love them even after their death. Now this idea of soul-consciousness after death was believed by the Egyptians, and yet not one of their superstitions became mixed with Judaism.

First Samuel 28:12–19 tells the story of beleaguered King Saul speaking with Samuel long after the latter had died. Apart from all the puzzles in this story, several things are clear. (1) Saul and most others believed that Samuel was conscious after death. (2) God allowed Samuel to appear and reveal super-human knowledge to Saul. (3) Events that followed verify the genuineness of Samuel's existence after death. (4) The prevalence of necromancers, or mediums, or familiar spirits, was recognized in spite of divine disapproval.

Psalm 16:10 is recognized by Paul (Acts 13:35) as referring to the resurrection of Christ, but it is also an indication of soul consciousness after death. Psalm 73:24 indicates that at death the righteous will be received into glory. Psalm 86:13 says, "thou hast delivered my soul from the lowest Sheol."

Ecclesiastes 12:7 seems to show that Solomon came back to his right mind, after having been skeptical previously. He wrote, "and the dust returneth to the earth as it was, and the spirit returneth unto God who gave it." These two events would occur simultaneously.

Isaiah 14:9, 10 tells of those in Sheol as conscious and talking. Some scholars believe that Isaiah 38:17 speaks of souls in Sheol as being conscious. More definite is Ezekiel 32:21, "The strong among the mighty shall speak to him out of Sheol with them that help him."

6. *The New Testament Is Clear on Soul Consciousness after Death.*

In John 11:26 Jesus promised, "and whosoever liveth and believeth on me shall never die." Since believers die physically as do unbelievers, this verse must necessarily mean that the souls of believers will never die, and that they retain consciousness between death and resurrection. What else can such clear promises mean?

This writer, as most pastors, has often used 2 Corinthians 5:1-10 in comforting believers at funerals of their loved ones. The promise is clear: when this body dies, "we have a building from God, a house not made with hands, *eternal* in the heavens. For verily in this we groan, longing to be clothed upon with our habitation which is from heaven . . . we would be clothed upon, that what is mortal may be swallowed up of life. Now he that wrought us for this very thing is God, who gave unto us the earnest of the Spirit." Comment: would God give us the Spirit on earth, and then separate us from Him at death? When God in John 3:16 promises us *everlasting* life, would He terminate that spiritual life at death? No.

Now 2 Corinthians 5:6, "knowing that, whilst we are at home in the body, we are absent from the Lord" (physically, that is). V. 8, "We are willing rather to be absent from the body, and to be at home with the Lord." How could any promise be clearer than this, that absence from the body means presence with the Lord? Knowing something of God's infinite grace, it seems right that it should be so.

"For me to live is Christ, and to die is gain . . . having a desire to depart and be with Christ; for it is very far better" (Phil. 1:21, 23). This passage indicates that being with Christ will follow immediately after the death of believers.

"Whether we wake or sleep, we should live together with him" (1 Thes. 5:10)—that is, with our Lord Jesus. Hebrews 12:23 speaks in the present tense of "the general assembly and church of the firstborn who are enrolled in heaven, and to God the Judge of all, and to the spirits of just men made perfect."

Peter tells us (1 Peter 3:19) of the unsaved "spirits in prison, that aforetime were disobedient" but now are capable of communicating.

In Revelation 6:9-11 we have the spirit world unveiled. (The Book of Revelation is not for obscuring or obfuscation; it is instead an unveiling.) "I saw underneath the altar the souls of them that had been slain for the Word of God, and for the testimony which they held: and they cried with a great voice, saying,

How long, O Master, the holy and true, dost thou not judge and avenge our blood on them that dwell on the earth? And there was given to each one a white robe; and it was said unto them, that they should rest yet for a little time, until their fellow-servants also and their brethren, who should be killed even as they were, should have fulfilled their course." It is clear that this scene took place before the resurrection, and after the physical deaths of those involved.

Revelation 7:13–17 is quite as clear in showing the consciousness of those believers who had died and were happily serving God before their actual resurrection. They are arrayed in white robes, indicating perfect cleansing from all the sins of earth, and their sufferings are all at an end. Then we who now believe in Christ need not expect an indefinite era of utter oblivion, but rather immediate acceptance into the presence of our Redeemer. Like dying Stephen who saw the Lord Jesus standing as if to welcome him into heaven, so we may believe an immediate reception into glory awaits us at our death.

Visiting several death beds during my ministry, I have heard the last words of the dying who spoke of seeing the glorified Christ. Even so, D. L. Moody on a Friday at twelve noon, December 22, 1899, said to his loved ones in a clear voice, "If this is death, there is no valley. This is glorious. I have been within the gates, and I saw the children! Earth is receding; Heaven approaching. God is calling me!" Then his eyes turned toward his wife Emma—she who had, next to Christ, been dearest of all to him—and he whispered the words that sang in her bereaved heart the four lonely remaining years—"You have been a GOOD wife to me!"

(The above was read at a meeting of the Evangelical Theological Society on April 17, 1970, in Winona Lake, Indiana. Among the many scholars present during the subsequent discussion of the paper, none expressed any disagreement with soul-consciousness after death.)

* * *

Mr. Garner Ted Armstrong (GTA) would disagree with the above. In his tract he refers to "confusion" of "religionists" who, in his opinion, are all mixed up. He drags a "red herring" by citing cases of massaging the hearts of "dead" persons and thus "restoring" life; then he asks, "Where were they during their deaths?" They were not dead! He tries to show that the Old

Testament word for soul, *nephesh,* is also used of animals, implying that man IS a soul and that he does not *have* a soul. But GTA is careless with the facts (Gen. 27:4, 19, 25, 31; Isa. 1:14; 51:23; 53:10; Psalm 16:10). And he contradicts himself; he says *nephesh* always speaks of animal life which means oxygen carried by the blood, yet in another place he says *nephesh* refers to a dead body!

As with a great many words, the word "soul" has different meanings, depending on the context. GTA picks out one meaning that suits his purpose, and he tries to apply it to other cases in order to support his heresy.

Then GTA raises a smoke screen by trying to show that the idea of immortality came from pagan Greeks. It did not; the Bible never was dependent upon any pagan philosophy or speculation.

GTA quotes Ecclesiastes 3:19 about a man dying like a beast; he should also read 3:21 which says, "Who knoweth the spirit of man that goeth upward, and the spirit of the beast that goeth downward to the earth?" "Then shall the dust return to earth as it was, and the spirit shall return unto God, who gave it" (Eccl. 12:7).

Jesus promised "rest unto your souls" in Matthew 11:29, but this could not refer to either one's body or his natural life. Jesus asked, "What shall a man give in exchange for his soul?" (Matt. 16:26); this makes no sense if it refers to one's body which he will lose anyway.

Among other verses GTA should read are Luke 2:35; Acts 2:27; 4:32; 15:24; Romans 2:9; Hebrews 6:19; 10:39; 13:17; James 1:21; 5:20; 1 Peter 1:9, 22; 2:11; 4:19; 2 Peter 2:8, 14.

* * *

Recently I asked two young cultists to choose between these two: *Christ* said to the repentant, converted thief, "Verily I say unto thee, Today shalt thou be with me in paradise." So this new convert has *now* been in paradise-heaven for 1940 years so far, in perfect happiness.

Cultists say, "When you die, you are totally dead, as a dog dies. You will not be born again until the resurrection. You will not be in any kind of paradise, or heaven, right after your body dies. You must wait."

Choose which of these two you prefer.

32

LAZARUS AND
THE RICH MAN, REVISED

MR. H. W. ARMSTRONG (HWA) has a tract on "Lazarus and the Rich Man." Nowhere are his cunning gimmicks and errors more evident than here.

With a Bible open to Luke 16:19–31, count the mistakes, misrepresentations and subtle insinuations in this tract by HWA.

He says the churches and clergy use this account of Lazarus and the rich man more than any other to show that saved people go to heaven at death. Wrong; we much prefer passages such as John 5:28, 29; 14:1–3; Acts 7:55–60; 2 Corinthians 5:1–10; Philippians 1:20–23; 2 Timothy 4:6–8.

HWA promises that he will treat this passage literally. But he does NOT; he twists and spiritualizes and distorts and "interprets."

He says, with *no reason or Biblical basis*, that Lazarus is pictured as a Gentile, and thus represents all saved Gentiles. But Lazarus is a Jewish name (John 11:1 ff); it is *not* a Gentile name. It means "without help" and is found 15 times in the New Testament. How can anyone believe HWA who uses such a false assumption as a basis for his "interpretation." He is like an umpire who makes up his own rules at each ball game, or like the boy who needed an "8" to make his answer come out as he wanted!

HWA insists that God did not promise heaven to Abraham, but Christ said he was in the kingdom of *heaven* (Matt. 8:11).

HWA ignores this. Every indication is that the soul of Abraham is now in a place that can be called heaven, even as Christ promised paradise to the repentant thief.

HWA makes a big deal about Palestine being promised to Abraham (Gen. 12:5-7), and he tries to put Lazarus there. But Christ did not do that.

HWA insists that Lazarus became one of Abraham's children (but called a Gentile by HWA?), and thus an heir with Abraham of Palestine. But our Lord did not say that. Abraham's soul lives now with God and the angels, and that is where Christ said the soul of Lazarus was also.

HWA refers frequently to the "false teaching" of men, meaning all the intelligent, fruitful, Spirit-led Christians who have always believed what Christ *said,* instead of HWA's far-fetched interpretations.

Incidentally, HWA calls Stephen the first Christian martyr, but everyone knows that John the Baptist suffered martyrdom first. And John was as much a Christian as Stephen was. Both were real believers.

HWA says that Abraham was still dead, citing John 8:52. We know *his body* died, but Christ showed conclusively that our God is the God of the living—of Abraham, Isaac and Jacob (Matt. 22:32; Mark 12:26, 27; Luke 20:37, 38). More on this in our preceding chapter.

HWA says that Lazarus, "like Abraham," is still dead. But Christ said that though his body died, the real Lazarus was taken to the glory of Abraham's bosom. That means immortality; his soul did NOT die.

HWA lies when he says Lazarus *"is to be* carried." He makes a pretense of knowing Greek, but the Greek in this case is aorist, meaning *past* completed action. It is NOT future, and HWA must know this. It is clear that he is deliberately deceiving those who do not know Greek, or who do not bother to check up on his honesty.

He implies that angels will not come down from heaven until the future resurrection, but we all know that angels came before that (Matt. 1:20; 2:13, 19; Mark 1:13; Luke 1:11, 13, 18, 26, 30, 34, 38; 2:9-15; John 20:12; Acts 5:19; 8:26; 10:7; 12:7-23; 27:23.

Instead of his vaunted "plain truth," HWA uses a plain trick.

He says the *time* that the angels carry Lazarus into Abraham's bosom is at the future resurrection. But Christ said it was at the time of his death—*while the rich man's brothers were alive on earth!* Believe *Christ.*

Again HWA resorts to wily words. Now he tries to show that, in spite of Christ's plain statement, the rich man was not found in hell right after his death. But Christ said "the rich man also died, and was buried; and in hell he lifted up his eyes, being in torments" (Luke 16:22, 23).

HWA has the effrontery to say that the rich man was in the same kind of hell as Christ was in between His death and resurrection (Acts 2:31). But Hebrew teaching shows that hades was a place for the dead, with *two* parts. Thus Abraham and the rich man could converse, even across the "great gulf" between them.

HWA copies the heresy of Jehovah's Witnesses in saying that "hades" means the grave. It may sometimes, but not always. It does not mean the grave in Luke 16:19–31. Poor Lazarus likely had no burial in a grave.

HWA tries to deceive us by saying the rich man would not open his eyes until the resurrection. Again he cheats—knowingly or not—for the Greek word for "lifted" is *eparas,* aorist tense, which means past action *completed.* HWA must know that, but he has a false doctrine to support. He says the rich man will not open his eyes until after the millennium! But this is certainly *not* what Christ said.

HWA tries hard to show that souls are not conscious after death. He uses Jehovah's Witnesses' favorite texts. Quoting Ecclesiastes 9:5, "the dead know not anything," he implies that this proves his point. He fails to believe Christ instead of backslidden Solomon! Of course "John Doe," in his fresh grave, does not know who closed his tomb, or what people said about him! But John Doe's soul, as with Lazarus, knows whether he is in the good place or in the bad place. So will everyone.

By the same unfair means HWA tries to have Job and David bolster his heresy, but both were talking from their earthly stance.

Another deception of HWA is to say that many people have "died" and then by artificial means their hearts were started beating again. Of course such could not recall the next world;

they had not really died! But HWA wants us to think they did, even though death means there is no more physical life to restore.

HWA deceitfully converts the history of Luke 16:19–31 into prophecy. He does this by dishonestly changing past tenses into future tenses.

He says the rich man's tongue was dry because of fright at seeing the flames all around him. So his suffering was merely fright, not the fire! HWA says he broke out in a *cold sweat!* (Then he had more moisture than Lazarus' finger-tip could carry.) And he says this fire would burn him up, destroying him completely. Yet he admits that Christ did not say how long his suffering would last. But HWA seems too positive about matters not revealed at all. The "gulf" is immortality, he says. And he says fire consumes the body *before* the person dies. Hardly.

HWA says the rich man knew Lazarus had been resurrected. False. And he says this whole account is given to prove the fact of the resurrection—but the resurrection is not the issue here.

HWA tries desperately to turn this story of death into a story of future resurrection. But Abraham said that the rich man's brother would not believe *"though* one rose from the dead." The word "though" is *ean,* "if," coupled with the subjunctive verb *anaste.* So resurrection is not the question here.

Most damaging to HWA's frantic and futile "reconstruction" of Lazarus and the rich man is the fact that the rich man had five brothers living on earth *at the very time* he himself was speaking to Abraham. This demolishes the inventions of Armstrong decisively.

But HWA is equally self-deceived about Enoch and Elijah. Next.

33

ENOCH AND ELIJAH DIED, SAYS ARMSTRONG

Mr. Herman L. Hoeh, writing for Armstrong, begins his tract on Enoch and Elijah by quoting John 3:13, "And no man hath ascended up to heaven, but he that came down from heaven, even the Son of man who is in heaven." More accurate is the rsv: No one has ascended into heaven but he who descended from heaven, the Son of man. Mr. Hoeh assumes that one verse may apply in all contexts different from its own. He breaks a rule that says an obscure text must not determine the meaning of similar texts which are very plain. So he keeps Enoch and Elijah out of heaven! He should read 2 Peter 1:20, "no prophecy of the scripture is of any private interpretation."

The familiar Lord's Prayer begins, "Our Father who art *in heaven.*" And since Genesis 5:24 says of Enoch that "God took him," why not believe that he went to be with God in heaven? But not Mr. H; he says that Enoch is dead as any animal or man. He must bolster his errors somehow.

Mr. Hoeh insists that Enoch must have died. But Hebrews 11:5 says no; "Enoch was translated that he should *not see death,* and was not found . . ." He left the earth without dying. God took him. Mr. Hoeh quoted Hebrews 11:5 but omitted the part, "he should not see death."

Then Mr. Hoeh tries to compare Enoch with Jacob in Acts 7:16. On this unfair basis he says that God took Enoch and buried him. Does your Bible say that? Not mine. Nor Armstrong's. Mr. Hoeh cannot be trusted.

174

Next Mr. Hoeh refers to Moses whose burial place no one ever knew, so "he was not found" either. What a trick! With it, Mr. Hoeh wants us to believe that Enoch died as Moses did.

And Mr. Hoeh gets all mixed up. He refers to Colossians 1:13, "hath *translated* us into the kingdom of his dear Son." What if this Greek word is used in Acts 7:16 and Hebrews 11:5? Its meaning depends on its context. And Colossians 1:13 DOES say we are NOW saved and NOW in the kingdom.

On the misread basis of Hebrews 11:39, Mr. Hoeh insists that Enoch has not yet inherited eternal life, and will not do so until Christ comes again. Then Mr. Hoeh accuses Paul of saying that Enoch died!

But now he notices the phrase "should not see death" (Heb. 11:5). He says *this* death does not mean the first (physical) death, but a later one as in John 8:51 and 11:26. But the Bible *does not say that!* And every saved person in the Old Testament could escape this "second death," so that Mr. Hoeh's argument has not the slightest basis in fact.

Mr. Hoeh assumes, without ANY facts, that Enoch's first 65 years of life were in sin and darkness. Not one verse says that.

More errors: Mr. Hoeh says God took Enoch just as He took Moses; that God buried Enoch; that Enoch's "second translation" was death; and that Enoch still awaits the resurrection.

All these devious Armstrongish detours are made to keep departed believers (including our own deceased loved ones) out of heaven now. Armstrongism wants them all dead as dogs for now—a long, long now.

Next, Mr. Hoeh tries to dispose of Elijah. He refers to three heavens, and assumes that Elijah could not be in God's heaven, but only in the earth's upper atmosphere! Why? Because only in this lower heaven can whirlwinds occur! Mr. Hoeh says that! So he limits the Almighty. He is that determined not to admit Elijah's immortality—until Christ's return. If Elijah did not die then, Mr. Hoeh thinks he would have preeminence over Christ. If that isn't strange thinking, what is?

So why was Elijah taken up? Only to give Elisha "first place!"

And where did Elijah go? Not to the throne of God, Mr. Hoeh says.

And Mr. Hoeh tries to tell us that Elijah continued living on earth "some place." He cites a letter (2 Chron. 21:12-15) which of course Elijah wrote before his departure, but which Mr. Hoeh wants us to think was written about ten years later from "another" location.

Perhaps Mr. Hoeh got some of his ideas from the doubting "sons of the prophets" in 2 Kings 2:15-18.

> "And when the sons of the prophets, who were looking on (Elisha, after Elijah's departure). . . . they said to Elisha, Behold, now, there are with thy servants fifty strong men; let them go, we pray thee, and seek thy master (Elijah), lest perhaps the Spirit of the Lord hath taken him up, and cast him upon some mountain, or into some valley.
>
> "And he' said, Ye shall not send. And when they urged him till he was ashamed, he said, Send. They sent therefore, fifty men; and they sought three days, but found him not. And when they came again to him (for he tarried at Jericho), he said unto them, Did I not say unto you, Go not?"

So. Mr. Hoeh now has Elisha to contend with, too. Elisha would not believe Mr. Hoeh; why should we? Try telling Elisha that Elijah has been dead as a dog in a grave 2800 years! Mr. Hoeh would get clobbered!

But Armstrongites challenge God Himself. Garner Ted shows how.

34

GARNER TED ARMSTRONG
CHALLENGES GOD!

GARNER TED HAS a tract, "Who—What—Was Jesus before His Human Birth?" In it he denies that it was the Heavenly Father who spoke to His Son in Matthew 17:5, "This is my beloved Son, in whom I am well pleased; hear ye him." GTA says it must have been an angel with a message from heaven.

But no angel could speak about Christ as his (an angel's) Son!

NO ONE but the Heavenly Father could say Christ was His Son.

GTA cites John 5:37 as "proof" for his erratic assertion, "Ye have neither heard his (the Father's) voice . . ." But this verse was spoken at least one year before Matthew 17:5. And it is not fair to make one verse apply to every possible context. No verse is of "*private*" interpretation.

The Armstrong cultists fail to understand 2 Peter 1:20. They fail to compare Scripture with Scripture (1 Cor. 2:13-15). They love to take one verse and make it apply mechanically to all other verses having something in common. They lack Hermeneutics. They seem to have no discernment, especially as to interpreting difficult verses in the light of others which are much clearer.

To assert that God did not speak in Matthew 17:5 is denying God and the plain truth. It is folly, and a dogmatic assumption of superior wisdom.

GTA is also sure that it was NOT God the Father who spoke

to Moses in Exodus 33:12-23. Yet God then told Moses, "there shall no man see me, and live" (v. 20). That is basic. But GTA says it was the pre-incarnate Christ who spoke to Moses. But Christ was seen face to face later by multitudes of people, both friends and foes! GTA is wrong again.

No wonder it is hard to believe anything GTA says or writes.

He denies that the God of the Old Testament was the Father of Christ, quoting 1 Corinthians 10:4 which is irrelevant. But Christ spoke repeatedly of His Father as the God of the Old Testament (John 2:16; 4:21, 23; 5:17, 20).

Worse, GTA says it was possible for Christ to sin and become lost forever! How terrible! Hebrews 13:8 says Christ is "the same yesterday, and today, and forever." If GTA is right, Christ could sin now! Awful! And since it is impossible for God to lie (Heb. 6:18), so it was then impossible for Christ to lie or sin any other way.

Trust the Bible's clear statements, not Armstrong's "confusionism." The Pasadena presses pour out persistent propaganda, so we must continue turning the Bible's searchlight on their many blunders.

Now comes the shocking, ultimate blasphemy!

35

ARMSTRONGITES WANT
TO BECOME GODS!

HERE IS THE ultimate bait held out to Armstrongites. (It is also ultimate blasphemy!) In *Tomorrow's World,* April, 1971, Robert L. Kuhn wrote on "What It Means to be Equal with God." So now Armstrongism knows all about God, since they tell how to be EQUAL with Him! Then either their god is too small, or they are too big for heaven. Either their god is no longer infinite, or Armstrongites will no more be finite. But—

"He who sitteth in the heavens shall laugh; the Lord shall have them in derision" (Psalm 2:4). ". . . (the antichrist) as God, sitteth in the temple of God, showing himself that he is God" (2 Thes. 2:4).

"I will be like the Most High" said Lucifer in Isaiah 14:14.

The devil himself, when he was still called Lucifer, fell for this Armstrong-like bait (Isa. 14:12-14; Ezek. 28:12-19). "I will be like the Most High" was the rebellious, ambitious, blasphemous, arrogant, and lustful desire that turned Lucifer into Satan. It meant his eternal ruin. Ever since, that old serpent has been trying to ruin as many as possible. He started with Eve.

"Yea, hath God said?" Satan asked Eve, getting her to doubt the clear revelation of God. Even so, Armstrongism tempts people to doubt the plain word of God, plus doubting most of the world's Spirit-filled, intelligent, and prayerful Bible scholars.

"Ye shall be as God," Satan told Eve. Armstrong raises that bid; he bids higher for modern Eves and Adams; he outbids

179

Satan himself. "You SHALL BE God," says Armstrong, "exactly like God!" This blatant blasphemy is also in the tract, "Why Were You Born?" on page 21.

But God never has had, and never will have, an equal. Armstrongites tell a *devilish lie* when they say any human being will ever be God.

"Thou shalt have *no other gods before me*" (Exo. 20:3) is the first commandment, repeated in the New Testament. "Before" means "in the presence of." But Armstrong wants equality with *God!*

God explains *why* He gave this first commandment. ". . . for I, the Lord thy God, am a jealous God . . ." (Exo. 20:5). "Jealous" here means unique, exacting *exclusive* devotion, intolerant of rivalry. "For thou shalt worship no other god; for the Lord, whose name is Jealous, is a jealous God" (Exo. 34:14). See also Deut. 4:24; 5:9; 6:15 for more on *what God says* about Armstrong's arrogant blasphemy.

"My glory will I not give to another" (Isa. 42:8).

"I am God, and there is none else" (Isa. 45:22).

"And I will not give my glory to another" (Isa. 48:11).

Yet Armstrong insolently defies the plain truth of the Bible. He tells Almighty God, "Move over; I shall be equal with you!!!" (Not a quotation.)

When the Bible says that our God is jealous, it means that he is anxious for our welfare. Since He is the Source of all good, then for us to leave Him for another god, or even share another god with Him, is an infinite loss to us. He wants the very best for us, just as a good husband wants the very best for his wife. If she flirts with another man she is flirting with danger, distress, divorce, and disaster.

While it is true that we Christians are called "children of God," it is NOT true that we shall ever be equal with God. I would not want that responsibility. Most of us find it hard enough to manage our own affairs, but not Armstrong. He wants to "counsel" God too!

Our blessed Lord Jesus who IS God "thought it not robbery to be equal with God" (Phil. 2:6). But now Armstrong elevates himself, and tries to get others, into that Deity which God will never "share with another."

Whatever joys and honors God has for us in the future, we

shall always be—compared to Him—in a different genre, species or category. And Armstrongites are on very dangerous ground when they teach otherwise.

God is "A Spirit infinite, eternal, and unchangeable in His being, wisdom, power, holiness, justice, goodness, and truth" (Westminster Catechism). God is the "eternal, uncaused, independent, necessary Being, that hath active power, life, wisdom, goodness, and whatsoever other supposable excellency, in the highest perfection, in and of itself" (John Howe). God is omnipotent, omnipresent, omniscient, "MOST high" (Acts 7:48).

God does not reproduce *Himself*. He never will. No verse says He will.

Armstrong's idea of a "God-family" is a Mormon invention. No such family is found in the Bible. Armstrong tries to push the Holy Spirit out of the Trinity, and now he wants to push himself in.

Mr. Kuhn tries to destroy the Trinity by saying that only two Persons were active in the creation. Yet Genesis 1:2 mentions the Spirit as sharing in the work of creation. See also Job 26:13; 33:4; Psalm 104:30. He also says the Hebrew word "Elohim" in Genesis 1:1 is plural, meaning two—Father and Son only. But the Hebrew language also has the *dual* form for numbers, meaning only two. Genesis 1:1 does NOT have the dual form!

It is plain blasphemy for Armstrongites to teach that they will ever act, feel, or have experiences at the same level with God. Such teaching is preparing the way for the awful Antichrist, the man of sin, "the son of perdition, who opposeth and exalteth himself above all that is called God, or that is worshipped . . ." (2 Thes. 2:3, 4).

In apparent desperation for more and bigger bait to win followers, to *outbid all other cult leaders*, and even to outbid Satan himself, Armstrong promises his prospects that they will some day *advise* and *counsel* God Himself! Literally incredible. (*Tomorrow's World*, April, 1971, p. 45).

More—and worse! Mr. Kuhn says we will give our suggestions and opinions to help God manage all "reality." And Mr. Kuhn is not modest at all. *His* opinions and ideas will be both unique and original. So now he is about to out-think God! Next step: depose God.

Since Armstrong admits that 60% of his converts are women,

then 60% of his future gods will be "Mrs. Gods!" This is his to-morrow's world!

Armstrong dares to say that he and his will be changed into literal God Beings, as much as God the Father, exactly like God. But the Holy Spirit? He is only an "it"! Abhorrent blasphemy!

If the Armstrongites become "equal with God," then the Bible must be changed, and *God's Name changed* from "the MOST HIGH God" as it is now in Mark 5:7; Luke 8:28; Acts 7:48; 16:17; Hebrews 7:1. Then "The MOST HIGH God" will only be "an average God," along with all the Mr. and Mrs. "Gods" of Armstrongism. Incredible? Yes.

"And for this cause" (rejection of Bible facts) "God shall send them *strong delusion,* that they should believe a lie" (2 Thes. 2:11).

This strong delusion has now come. It is here, and growing daily. Armstrongism now teaches the lie first told by the devil himself. (Mormons also teach that Adam is now god, etc. They have many gods.)

But of the scores of cults, Armstrongism is the most blasphemous.

This is the ultimate, a climax. What follows in our remaining chapters may seem anticlimactic, yet we think they are important. For this new false cult seeks to control one's entire life, even one's birthdays. If they control such minor matters, then they are slave drivers indeed.

"Be not entangled again with the yoke of bondage" (Gal. 5:1).

36

BIRTHDAYS—ANOTHER ARMSTRONG TABOO

THE ARMSTRONG HIERARCHY is not satisfied to impose only old Jewish laws upon their proselytes and dependents; they must also add more rules of their own invention. As for taboos, it seems that the more primitive a tribe is, the more superstitions and taboos they have. Anthropologists and missionaries have found a great many taboos, most of them ridiculous and some even dangerous.

An Armstrongite, Kenneth C. Herrman, has a tract entitled "Should Christians Celebrate Birthdays?" This cult also forbids the use of pork products and other foods forbidden to Israel but permitted to New Testament Christians. They also forbid their people to attend our good churches, especially on Sundays. What will they think of next?

Regarding taboos and asceticism, Paul had very sensible thoughts—

> If you died with Christ to the world's rudimentary notions, why, as if you still lived in the world, do you submit yourselves to dogmatisms founded on teachings and doctrines of men—such as "Do not handle this," "You must not taste that," "Do not touch this"—all things which are intended to perish in the using? For these precepts, although they have a show of wisdom with their self-imposed devotions and fastings and bodily austerities, are of no real value against the indulgence of the carnal appetites (Col. 2:20-23).
>
> —Centenary Translation

183

It seems that Armstrong delights in taking many joys out of life. Why impose needless taboos on Christmas, Easter, Sundays, New Year's Day, good food, and now birthdays? His odd reason for birthday taboos: the only two birthday celebrations in the Bible were for Pharaoh in Genesis 40:20 and Herod in Matthew 14:6. Then why not also prohibit banquets, since wicked Belshazzar had one (Daniel 5)?

Not even Mosaic laws forbade birthdays. *The Living Bible* on Job 1:4—"Every year when each of Job's sons had a birthday, he invited his brothers and sisters to his home for a celebration."

Should we not rejoice that a loved one has had one more year of life with useful living? Why not be thankful that God has given us another year of privileges? Why not rejoice, especially at anniversaries, over God's *continued* goodness to us?

At Christ's birth the angels rejoiced. So did the shepherds, the wise men, Anna, Simeon, Mary, Joseph, Zacharias, Elizabeth, and all believers. As to the exact date of His birth, no matter. Since kings and queens can set official dates, other than the actual, for their birthdays, what is so evil about December 25? Who knows, or cares, about any pagan affair on or about that date? Loving Christ, we love Christmas.

But Armstrong wants *complete* allegiance to himself and to his laws.

Mr. K. C. Herrman (KCH), as other Armstrongites, reverts to backslidden Solomon in Ecclesiastes 7:2, "It is better to go to the house of mourning, than to go to the house of feasting." Such reasoning is like the man who wanted a Bible verse for suicide. He read about Judas hanging himself and then read in a different setting, "Go, and do thou likewise."

And Job cursed the day of his birth (Job 3:3), as though we are to follow his example in such self-pity! Must we blame God for *life?* But Job's extreme sufferings were some excuse for his unnatural remarks.

Mr. KCH refers to Josephus and some old Jewish laws (non-Biblical) about festivals for the births of children, but why should we be bound by such pointless prohibitions?

He says our December 25th celebrations came from paganism. If the date coincides, what matter? We have no paganism in our happy Christian festivities. We do not need Santa Claus, kind and lovable as "he" is, for he may eclipse the real Christ, if even a little. But we do like our Christmas carols, the music, the merriment, the greetings of "Merry Christmas," the lovely cards, the visits, the programs, the lights, the presents, and all the good will overflowing. We feel more love to God and to men for all this *pure* Christmas spirit.

But Armstrongism would rob from all our children the many innocent joys of the day when Christ is so universally honored. We would gladly discard Santa Claus entirely if that would bring more honor to Christ our Savior. But we refuse to "throw out the baby with the bath water."

Mr. KCH says we are to observe the day of Christ's death (which we do) instead of the day of His birth (which is not forbidden).

And he blames us for using the Roman calendar. Ho, hum. What next?

Now get this: "the day of death (is better) than the day of one's birth" (Eccl. 7:1). KCH says this is a correct appraisal of the day of our birth! So he joins backslidden, blinded Solomon. Then Armstrongites should rejoice over war's casualties, over all funerals, all fatal accidents, all obituaries, all heart failures, terminal cancers, etc.!

Then a loving mother could look at her sleeping baby and say, "I was very glad for your birth, but now Armstrong says the day of your death will be better." She could look at her husband and say, "I used to celebrate your birthdays, but no more; the day of your death will be better." And to her loving parents, "The days of your deaths will be better than your birthdays." To brothers and sisters, "No more birthday festivities for you; the days of your deaths will be better. Armstrong says so; that's who says so. He also says you will die like beasts; you will be as dead as animals until the resurrection."

What a ghoulish, garish, gruesome "gospel" is Armstrongism!

Glorious contrast: "Many shall rejoice at his birth" (Luke 1:14). And since we were not there at the time, we can rejoice now. But this joy was over John the Baptist. *How much greater* is our joy over Christ's birth. This was *"good tidings of great joy, which shall be to all people"* (Luke 2:10).

Is once· a year too often to celebrate Christ's birth?

Or our own?

But like "Big Brother" in George Orwell's book *1984*, the Armstrong people want to watch you and regulate you in a great many miscellaneous matters of your life.

37

LETTERS AND MISCELLANY

I HAVE WRITTEN several letters to the Armstrong headquarters, asking permission to quote from their publications. After a long delay, a letter came imposing very difficult conditions. It is clear that they do not want anyone to expose their many fallacies.

Having written nine books previously, I have sent scores of letters to other publishers and have always received permission courteously. But now I must limit verbatim references to two or three words. Allusions to their writings have been carefully made, and not out of context.

The Armstrongites are not allowed to meet without an official agent present. They want no outsiders to attend their "services." They seem to be afraid of intelligent inquirers. One agent said that some people might come and disrupt a meeting! I replied, "I have been going to meetings of Christians for 50 years, and never saw one disrupted." But like a debutante, they play "hard to get." It is their psychological trick of arousing curiosity, and a desire to join their "inner circle." Later, I did "crash" their meetings.

But I have read a great many of their articles and therefore know what they do teach. Having graded thousands of examination papers on college and seminary levels (during my teaching career), I can say candidly that I learned how to detect errors, fallacies, deceptions and heresies.

Herbert W. Armstrong (HWA) was once affiliated with a

Stanberry, Missouri, (now based in Denver) group of Seventh
Day Church of God people. Their magazine, *The Bible Advocate,*
is in its 109th year, while Armstrong's is only in its 39th. The two
are very similar, even to titles of articles printed and those
offered free to inquirers. Now which copied from the other?
Each disowns the other, but they are surely kin.

A friend's letter to HWA asked, "Where in the Bible is a
Christian called a fetus?" A Mr. C. O. Huse replied, "We are
now *potential* heirs of God's Kingdom, but we are not physically
present within the Kingdom, and won't be until we are born of
the Spirit to be Spirit as 1 Corinthians explains." Corrections on
this: We are NOW heirs, not potential heirs (Rom. 8:17). We
are NOW in the Kingdom (Col. 1:13). We are NOW born of
the Spirit (John 3:8; 1 Peter 1:23).

Mr. Huse's first letter evaded the question, "Where in the
Bible is a Christian called a fetus, or even alluded to as such?"
A second letter repeated this question, "Where in the Bible is a
Christian called a fetus, or even alluded to as such?" plus "Why
do you say that a Christian is begotten by God's Spirit at the
time of baptism?" No answer!

Another letter to Ambassador College—"You say on pages 21,
22 of your tract, 'Why Were You Born?', 'You will actually BE
GOD, even as Jesus was and is God, and His Father, a different
Person, also is God! . . . You are setting out on a training to
become creator—to become God!' But God says (Isa. 45:5) 'I am
the Lord, and there is no other; besides me there is no God.'
How does this square with the assertion that resurrected Christians shall be Gods? If we are to become God, does this mean
that we will be worshipped as Gods in eternity?"

Do the Armstrongs actually expect to be worshipped as Gods
hereafter?

Mr. Armstrong prophesied in his *Plain Truth* of May, 1965,
p. 21, "The Arabs will control Jerusalem until the second coming
of Christ." Only two years later, during the six-day war of June,
1967, the Jews proved HWA to be a false prophet.

In his *Plain Truth* of May, 1964, HWA says the pagan gods
of ancient Egypt called "Amen" and "On" were Jesus Christ
(p. 44); that Cheops (Khufu) lived between 1726-1487 BC
(about 1300 years wrong). Job was Cheops (p. 45). Joseph
helped Cheops (Job) build the Great Pyramid at Gizeh (p. 46).

In his April, 1963 issue, p. 10, he wrote that God did not cause our Lord Jesus to re-enter the same body in which He died. But He DID (John 2:19-21; Luke 24:37-39; John 20:24-29).

And the Armstrong advice is not to vote. Why? Christ did not vote! Well, who could then? And did He use radios and write tracts?

"Where is the wise? Where is the scribe? Where is the disputer of this world? Hath not God made foolish the wisdom of this world? . . . not many wise men after the flesh, not many mighty, not many noble, are called" (1 Cor. 1:20–26).

Armstrong actually uses the above verses to try and cancel, or wipe out, all arguments against them by educated people! But—

There are some people who think there is virtue in ignorance; that the less you know, the more likely God can use you in His work.

When the Apostle Paul decried knowledge and wisdom, it was NOT that of the Lord, but of the world.

God does not make known His truth to men who deliberately ignore His Word. If HWA has some strange revelation about the new birth apart from the Bible, why does he depend on Bible proof texts for his teaching on any doctrine? Like other cultists, he builds doctrine without the Bible.

If wisdom and knowledge are disdained in God's sight, why does Armstrong emphasize study so much? Why does he indoctrinate his followers? Why does he have three colleges, correspondence courses, etc.?

If sound scholarship is something to avoid, perhaps we ought to cease referring to the Greek New Testament and lexicons which have come to us from great scholars. Ignorant men have contributed nothing to the books we use for help in understanding the Bible.

If true scholarship is characterized by avoiding the truth and neglecting the facts, how can one trust anything that Armstrong writes?

❊   ❊   ❊

One confirmed Armstrongite, in defending his position, cited Matthew 10:35, "For I am come to set a man at variance against his father, and the daughter against her mother, and the daughter-in-law against her mother-in-law." This is typical of

Armstrongism; they cite a verse out of context and suddenly they know more than all their previous teachers! Christ did not come just to divide families! And this same victim of Armstrongism suggested twice that I send for their literature!

❀ ❀ ❀

Of course I have read a great pile of Armstrong's tracts. HWA IS a clever, cunning, conniving scribe. After 60 years of experience in writing persuasive advertising, he can produce polished products. But God warns us "That we henceforth be no more children, tossed to and fro, and carried about with every wind of doctrine, by the sleight of men, and cunning craftiness, by which they lie in wait to deceive" (Eph. 4:14).

But Armstrong's writing is mostly spent in showing how "ignorant" the vast majority of Christian scholars are, and in contrast how suddenly a great wealth of knowledge is uniquely his. His skill is also shown in leading his victims to feel that they are sharing his extraordinary wisdom. This psychological device makes his people feel superior, just as he intended they should.

Imagine a prospective proselyte who has a "hang-up" on the sabbath question. He learns that Armstrong has written much about it, and he can get the "plain truth" without cost. So he sends for it; he reads, he believes it; he feels he has made a personal discovery, by himself; he has "made up his own mind"; he is thinking for himself (he thinks). "This is it. Eureka! I have found the truth at last." And he is completely insulated from all reason and Scripture proofs from then on.

This proselyte who wanted to be bound by sabbath laws reminds us of a young daughter of the English art critic, Mr. Duveen. At the ocean one day, he could not persuade her to join him in the chilly water. So he built a fire, heated a bucket of water, and then poured it into the ocean. Then the child ran gleefully into the ocean without hesitation. This father's trick, while harmless, is an illustration of how Satan often works. He mixes a small amount of truth into an ocean of falsehood, and people wade into it, not realizing how they have been deceived. (Adapted from *Our Daily Bread*, May 21, 1971, by Herbert Vander Lugt.)

❀ ❀ ❀

Some of Armstrong's tracts will twist words out of their real meanings.

Like—a farmer who sued his wife for a divorce. "Do you have

any grounds?" the judge asked. "Just a few acres." "Do you have a grudge?" was the next judicial query. "Yes, sir, but it's not big enough for but one car." Judge: "Does she beat you up?" "No, sir; I get up a whole hour before she does." Judge: "Is she a nagger?" "No, sir; she's white."

✿   ✿   ✿

When Herbert Armstrong was about 30, a popular song was about bubbles. He has built his doctrines on bubbles, easily punctured by Scripture points. Yet he keeps on blowing them, depending on his credulous converts to pay his big bills for radio, television and his colorful magazines.

Some Evils of Armstrongism	*Good in Gospel Churches*
Hurts soul-winning churches, Luke 11:52	Win real converts to Christ
Speaks against Holy Spirit, Matthew 12:32	Build real churches, hospitals
Slanders true Christians Matthew 5:10-12	Worldwide missionary work
Puts legalism in gospel, Galatians 3:1-5	Teach real Christian living
Destroys Sundays' joys, Colossians 2:16	Give Bibles in 1000 Languages
Twists Scriptures, 2 Peter 3:16	Give real Christian songs
Teaches false gospel, Galatians 1:7-9	Have real fruit of the Spirit
To be Gods in future, Isaiah 14:14	Lead to useful lives vs sin
Bondage to Jewish laws, Galatians 5:1-4	Live up to the New Testament

✿   ✿   ✿

Armstrong's correspondence courses are mostly a rehash of his tracts and magazine articles. In order to satisfy someone's possible curiosity, I read 30 of his 12-page "lessons" and found them crammed with propaganda, egotism, and attacks upon real Christians. To summarize them—

Lesson #1. Accuses Christians of "confusion"; meaning of gospel hidden until now, revealed only by H. W. Armstrong (HWA).

2. To announce future kingdom (Matt. 24:14) is more important than to win souls to Christ now (Matt. 28:19, 20; John 20:31). Churches are all in confusion; only HWA and his group have final answers!

3. HWA alone has "true" education; all else is mis-education. HWA's colleges are "God's" colleges. Precious few now obey God, except HWA people.

4. The coming Utopia, *a la* HWA. God's way is HWA's way, exclusively.

5. Tithing is recommended—if it benefits HWA's empire.

6. HWA, and only he, has the last word on Christ's Second Coming.

7. More on war. HWA is against it! He and the pope are for peace.

8. Natural disasters discussed; for rescue, see HWA. All bad in world is due to "Establishment" and churches; all good is HWA's Tomorrow's World.

9. HWA denies the Personality of the Holy Spirit (this blinds *him*).

10. HWA's church foretold in Revelation 3:7-13 as "Philadelphia" church.

11. A fairly good lesson against evolution. HWA has some good things.

12. HWA has absolute control of his colleges, so—"God controls them."

13. No promise of heaven to anyone converted now. Wait, says HWA.

14. No immortal souls now. Man "has no immortal soul," says HWA.

15. No real hell. Hell is only destruction of earth's surface!

16. "Born again" is not for now, not until the resurrection.

17. Obey the Ten Commandments, regardless of New Testament laws.

18. HWA mixes the Old and New Testament confusingly.

19. Only one true church: HWA's worldwide Church of God.

20. Holy Spirit is a force, not a Person, says HWA. (A dead spirit?)

21. Sick people disobey God by seeking doctors. (How about dentists?)

22. God is not trying to convert anyone now, says HWA. But He IS! "Seek ye the Lord while He may be found" (Isa. 55:6). "Repent, therefore, and *be converted,* that your sins may be blotted out" (Acts 3:19). "God . . . *now* commandeth all men everywhere to repent" (Acts 17:30).

23. HWA says the whole world is deceived in spiritual matters; most people do not know what the Holy Spirit is, what *it* is supposed to do. Millions believe in Christ but are not saved. Only 1400 years from Adam to Moses!

24. God won't accept you just as you are. Only right baptism is done by an HWA agent. Anyone questioning HWA is a "persecutor," he says.

25. Water baptism required for salvation. Dishonest comma in Luke 23:43.

26. Baptism must come before receiving the Holy Spirit, says HWA.

27. Holy Spirit given only to those keeping sabbaths! (But no verse tells any Gentile to keep any sabbath, in Old or New Testament.)

28. HWA and his kind are practicing to be Gods by worshipping on Saturdays. Christ was human exactly as we, could have eternal life only as we receive it! HE "had to" keep the sabbath or die eternal death! All churches but HWA's are unfruitful works of darkness, but HWA does not trust his own people to meet by themselves; one of his own ministers must be present.

29. Satan tempted Adam and Eve on Sunday, says HWA. Proof? None.

30. Beware the day of the sun! Satan caused sun and serpent to be associated together, in order to tempt people to honor Sundays. Roman Empire began 31 B.C.(!) Satan used Sunday to destroy mankind.

Caution to reader: the above are samples of some of HWA's lies. Do not let them linger in your memories; erase them with the Bible verses we have used to expose and demolish them. Memorize some of the verses in our chapter 39. They will be like a burst of sunlight after the dark clouds of Armstrong's legalism. Think on true, honest, just, pure, lovely things (Phil. 4:8).

❀   ❀   ❀

Extremely dangerous and alarming is Armstrong's "advice" on liquor in his October, 1971, *Plain Truth*, p. 28. He actually says there are "beneficial and balanced" uses of alcoholic drinks as with a good meal. This approval of alcohol negates an article filled with terrible facts on the horrible results of drinking. So HWA condones liquor which kills, cripples and ruins its millions annually. But he strictly forbids ham, bacon, or pork chops which, if properly prepared, never hurt anyone! He says that intoxicating liquor can be "beneficial" but not bacon! He suggests that if teetotaler parents condemn drinking, they risk rebellion in their children who may thus become "fanatical drinkers" with a wrong view of alcohol! Isn't such advice as bad as his theology?

* * *

Armstrongism would rob all children of the innocent joys of Hallowe'en (*Tomorrow's World*, Oct., 1971). He frightens his readers by conjuring up all sorts of hobgoblins, ghosts, and evil spirits of dead men which he identifies with this date. HWA is a master at telling ghost stories!

Valentine's day is also taboo—that happy day when people exchange heart-warming messages of love with friends, schoolmates, and relatives. HWA again plays Ghoul by digging up the graves of people he wants to use in ruining another happy day. He seems to hate Easter, Christmas, New Year's Day, all Sundays, and birthdays with demonic animosity. One wonders why. Is it to build up his Jewish feast days and sabbaths, none of which were ever commanded to any Gentile? He, or we, could dig up dirt galore to expose the heathenism back of his beloved "Saturndays."

Armstrong's many taboos against harmless pleasures demonstrate his strict *dictatorship* over his submissive followers.

* * *

What has made H. W. Armstrong so bitter against us Christians? Is it because of his triple failures, with his family suffering from hunger and cold, depending on their in-laws for a bare living? Is it because two other "ministers" fought him over a salary of $3 per week—and he lost? Is it to lure people who themselves have bitterness and resentment toward churches, pastors, or spouses? More than exposing communists, criminals, corrupt politicians, liquor makers and sellers, drug pushers, pornographic books, prostitutes, perverts, gangsters, atheists, and Bible-destroying liberals,—Mr. Armstrong attacks and belittles pastors and church people who are courteous, generous, kind, God-fearing, Christ-like, Spirit-filled, Bible-loving, and sacrificial soul winners.

And why does Armstrong advise his people against vaccinations, inoculations, and physicians (Correspondence Lesson #21)? Why not dentists? With smallpox almost conquered in our country, what sane person can doubt vaccination? Or the Salk vaccine against polio? Or tetanus shots? Or diphtheria antitoxin (which likely saved the life of our son at age three)? Yet Armstrongites, like Eddyites, trust their leader blindly and foolishly, risking their lives and the lives of their helpless children—all to obey an irrational cultist.

✿   ✿   ✿

As to date-setting, Mr. H. W. Armstrong had pinpointed January 7, 1972 as the precise time when his second 19-year cycle would end. He said, from Pentecost to Paul's going to, Europe was 19 years, and from then to the fall of Jerusalem was another 19 years. So, from HWA's first radio preaching January 7, 1934 to his first broadcast to Europe was 19 years, and then 19 more years should end his work on January 7, 1972. (Page 10 of A True History of the True Church.) On page 27 of this tract, we read that "God has given" this "church" of Armstrong *just two* 19-year periods in which to bring *his* gospel to the world. Thus each subservient, submissive follower of Armstrong is "stuck" with this prophecy. In June of 1971 an Armstrong minister tried, with considerable embarrassment, to evade this January 7, 1972 date of HWA's prophecy.

On page 10 of a blustering booklet, *1975 in Prophecy*, HWA predicted a really big drought "sooner than 1975"—perhaps between 1965 and 1972! Now who can blame us for doubting Armstrong? Are all his writers also false prophets? They all follow HWA with deferential meekness. The Bible tells us how to detect a false prophet. "When a prophet speaketh in the name of the Lord, if the thing follow not, nor come to pass, that is the thing which the Lord hath not spoken, but the prophet hath spoken it presumptuously; *thou shalt not be afraid of him*" (Deut. 18:22). No wonder that HWA has announced that his *1975 in Prophecy* is now taken out of circulation!

Should the Great Tribulation begin in 1972 or soon thereafter, it will not be due to HWA's guesses. The Bible does not give dates for future events, no matter what would-be "prophets" say to the contrary.

In his February, 1972, *Tomorrow's World*, HWA made some

lame excuses for his false prophecies. (1) He now says he is not a prophet—BUT he wrote *1975 in Prophecy* in 1957. (2) He says God has not revealed to him truths not found in the Bible—BUT he still insists on his Jeremiah-in-Ireland fantasy. (3) He says no one can be sure of dates—BUT he is still dogmatic on the Saturday-Resurrection in 31 A.D., and Pentecost on Monday! (4) He excuses his prophesied terminal date of January 7, 1972, by saying he did not know "how thoroughly" God wanted His future kingdom announced—BUT he still doesn't know! (5) He says his "gospel" is not after men—BUT he did get it from other cultists. (6) He does finally admit *a few* of his errors—BUT not his worst ones. (7) He says if he finds any more errors in his doctrine he will correct it—BUT many of us have told him of others he has not yet corrected. If he did, then Armstrongism would disappear!!

(8) To justify his work after 1-7-72, Armstrong adds non-biblical fantasies to Jeremiah's legendary career in Ireland and calls them FACT—But what sane historians says Jeremiah ever went there? (9) He says it is "established by prophecy" that Jeremiah started a third 19-year cycle—BUT no such "prophecy" exists in the Bible. Again, HWA is a false prophet. (10) It was *never* his intention, says HWA, to set dates—BUT it was, and he did! (11) He says about his book, *1975 in Prophecy*, that the date 1975 had nothing to do with prophecy—BUT it did! (12) He boasts of "getting the job done"—BUT attacking churches is a big part of his job. (13) He continues his serious error by saying the gospel is an announcement of a future kingdom—BUT the real gospel is salvation NOW by trusting Christ as Savior and Lord. (14) HWA tries hard to bail himself out of the January 7, 1972 date—his former terminal date—by planning more advertising, more buildings, and more radio propaganda—BUT his hundreds of blunders expose him as a continuing false prophet.

❖ ❖ ❖

A mother and baby froze to death in a terrible northern blizzard. It happened this way. They were on a train at night. The mother was very nervous lest she might miss her station where friends awaited her.

"Don't worry, ma'am," the conductor assured her. "I'll get you off at the right station. Just leave it all to me. This is my job."

A commercial man across the aisle overheard all this. Then—
"Lady, I know this road well. And the conductor has so much
to do, he may forget you. Your station is the one after the next
city. I'll be glad to help you."

When the next city was called the man said, "The next stop
is yours." When the train stopped next he said, "You see, the
conductor has forgotten you. I'll carry your baggage for you."
He also opened the door and let the woman and baby out into
the cold.

Shortly after, the conductor looked for the woman. "Where did
she go?" he asked. The false friend said, "You forgot her, but I
helped her off at the last stop."

"But that was not a station! That was an emergency stop! You
put her off in a wild area in this killing blizzard with no one to
meet her!"

Despite the danger to the entire train, they stopped and went
back several miles to search for the woman. After a long time
they found her, frozen to death in the snow, and the little baby
dead in her arms. Here were two victims of false information,
given by a foolish guide.

Anyone forsaking a gospel church for a self-appointed prophet
runs a great risk.

To make my research more authentic and complete, I
"crashed" a couple of Armstrong's meetings. I took careful notes
for I knew that some Armstrongites would like to prove me
wrong. But since I am not infallible, I have prayed much that
this work shall be fair and accurate. Honesty is the best policy.
My previous books and numerous magazine articles have all
been honest and unchallenged. "Provide things honest in the
sight of all men" (Rom. 12:17). Sir Henry Wotton wrote, "Tell
the truth, and so puzzle and confound your adversaries."

38

I "CRASH" TWO
ARMSTRONG MEETINGS

WISHING TO BE completely fair to Armstrongism, I asked one of their trained "ministers" to our house. (They do not want callers at their homes.) He brought a partner who said little. I had prepared questions.

Q. What could I gain by joining your Armstrong group? A. You would gain the sabbath and our feast days. What else? Indefinite, vague reply.

Q. What do you depend on for your salvation? A. I depend on Christ. Q. But you did that while you were a Baptist, before joining Armstrong. A. Now I also keep God's laws, such as the sabbath and the holy feasts. Q. And would you be lost if you stopped the sabbath-keeping. A. Yes, it would be the lake of fire for me then.

Q. Does continued salvation depend on loyalty to your group? A. It depends on my keeping the sabbath and the holy feasts (Leviticus 23).

Q. What is so new in Armstrong's teaching? A. The holy days, and no pagan holidays such as Christmas.

Q. How do you know Jeremiah went to Ireland, as Armstrong says? A. We have our representatives there who believe it is true. Q. But no authentic history books says it is true. A. We believe it is true.

Q. How do you know Jeroboam kept Sundays instead of the sabbaths, as Mr. Armstrong insists he did? A. A long frantic search in the Bible, but *he could not find one verse* to support this false claim.

Q. What do you expect to happen in 1972? A. Wait 8 years; you'll see. Q. But Armstrong's two 19-year cycles end in January, 1972; what will happen then? A. We don't know; wait 8 years. (We talked in June, 1971.)

Q. What is wrong with the *message* of Billy Graham? A. He does not recognize the sabbath, and he thinks the second coming of Christ is imminent. Q. Isn't it? A. No; Christ can not come for at least 3½ years, or until all of Revelation 6 to 17 has been fulfilled. Q. Find one verse to show He cannot come at any time, even today. A. After looking in Bible, *he could find none*.

Q. What reward do you expect to get for leading church members into your group? A. None. Q. Are you on salary? A. Yes. I spend my time calling on people who invite me into their homes to answer questions. Q What per cent of your converts are women? A. About 60 per cent.

Q. What has your group done in social welfare, compared to evangelical Christians who have built hospitals, orphanages, done pioneer missionary work and much other good work all over the world? A. We have had talks about ecology in India, Nepal, and Thailand.

Q. Where was your "Church of God" in 1921? A. In Oregon. Q. But that was before Mr. Armstrong got converted. A. In Oregon. Q. Where was your church in 1871? A. In England—a small group.

Q. What songs do you sing in your meetings? A. Mostly Psalms, but some songs from older hymn books. Q. Do you sing "Blessed Assurance?" A. We used to, but not any more; we don't like the sentiment in it.

Q. Where in the Bible is any Gentile told to keep the sabbath? A. I'll find it. (Frantic search in Bible 10 minutes; then request for larger concordance; intense search in Young's 1090 large-page concordance for 15 minutes; no success.) A. I'll find it in my own Bible and send it to you. (He did *not* send it to me. Six weeks later I asked him for his verse. Isaiah 56, he said. My reply: I know that passage; it has *no command* for any Gentile to keep the sabbath.)

Then I showed these two Armstrong agents that the sabbath commands were addressed to Israel specifically, and NEVER to any Gentile. No reply.

Next I asked where his sabbath meetings were held. Apparently flustered by his failures, and before realizing that he should not do it, he told me: 1622 Rand Road, N., Arlington Heights, Ill. I was *not* invited!

I went anyway, uninvited. The N. T. Churches did not have secret meetings (1 Cor. 14:23), and Jesus said, "In secret have I said nothing" (John 18:20).

Arriving at 2:00, Saturday, I saw about 300 people gathered. Several Psalms were sung. Then a sermonette, extolling their Texas spread. Many announcements: Sunday rummage sale pushed hard, to help headquarters; meetings and lectures announced; flute solo; then sermon until 4:00 on—

"Why We Don't Invite the Public to Our Sabbath Services."

There I was, uninvited, and now being told why! Well, I asked for it.

Some bits of 60-minute sermon: Our sabbath services are private; they are not tools of evangelism, but to instruct our converts. We won't throw anyone out, but we don't invite anyone not willing to go along with us. Misread 2 Corinthians 6:2, "Now is A day of salvation" instead of THE day." (See our chapter 20.) Sinners like Hitler can be saved hereafter. Christ did not try to win converts! Don't invite anyone; let us examine him and if he will go our way, we will invite him. Dr. M. F. Unger and H. H. Halley not converted! Only those God has called will go our way; we test them first.

My impressions: minister had sole control, as a dictator; no meetings allowed without him present; he took orders from headquarters. No spiritual vitality evident; like a political meeting.

I went again, three Saturdays later, to the same place, uninvited.

Sermonette told of airplane pilot who had to follow instructions, or lose his life; strong medicine—one drop kills! Application: follow all instructions from Armstrong or—the lake of fire. Then, lengthy promotion of rummage sale; headquarters needs more of your money. Then sermon—

"How to Keep the Sabbath" for 60 minutes. Isaiah 58:13, 14 used dishonestly; "If thou turn away thy foot from the sabbath, from doing thy *pleasure* on my holy day. . ." Speaker arbitrarily and dishonestly changed "pleasure" (Heb. *chephets)* to "business" *(melekah).* Also dishonest was his use of Exodus 35:3, "Ye shall kindle no *fire* throughout your *habitations* upon the sabbath day." He made "fire" such as Abraham carried in his hand to mean "a violent fire." And "habitations" he changed to "foundries."

Speaker would not pay his paper boy on Saturday, but he spent 15 minutes promoting Sunday sales! The sabbath command says to "not do ANY work" (Exo. 20:10) but speaker allows heating food, washing dishes, etc.

My impressions: dishonest, dictatorial, and dry. I don't want to return.

I telephoned the speaker 12 days later, asking him about his dishonest use of Exodus 35:3. "Look in your commentaries," was his repeated response. "I use the Bible as my authority." I said. Then I asked again for his promised verse on Jeroboam changing the sabbath, reminding him of his fruitless search in the Bible. "Now what is your answer?" He had none. He refused to come to my home. I meant to ask him why Armstrong said Christ was unconcerned about saving men's souls. Many verses say that Christ DID come to save souls (Matt. 20:28; 1:21; 18:11; Luke 7:50; 9:56; 19:10; 23:35; 1 Tim. 1:15, "Christ Jesus came into the world to save sinners. . ."

These apostates "received not the love of the truth, that they might be saved. And for this cause God shall send them *strong delusion,* that they should *believe the lie*" (2 Thes. 2:10, 11).

Now what should be our reaction, or response, to all heresies? It is to declare the truth as it is in the New Testament, soundly buttressed by the entire Bible.

The Old Testament law was given by Moses—and Armstrong, but *grace* and truth came by Jesus Christ (John 1:17).

Welcome, then, blessed Gospel of Grace!

39

FREE FROM THE LAW!
HALLELUJAH!

THIS CHAPTER COULD be sub-titled, "First Aid for Armstrongitis."

"For the law was given by Moses, BUT grace and truth came by Jesus Christ" (John 1:17). Notice, law and grace are different.

"And great GRACE was upon them all" (Acts 4:33).

"And by Him (Christ) all that believe are justified from all things, from which ye could not be justified by the law of Moses" (Acts 13:39).

"Paul . . . persuaded them to continue in the *grace* of God" (Acts 13:43).

"But we believe that through the *grace* of the Lord Jesus Christ we shall be saved, even as they" (Acts 15:11).

". . . to testify the gospel of the *grace* of God" (Acts 20:24).

"*Grace* to you and peace" (Rom. 1:7, as in all of Paul's epistles.)

"by the deeds of the law there shall no flesh be justified" (Rom. 3:20).

"righteousness of God apart from the law is manifested" (Rom. 3:21).

"Being justified freely *by his grace*" (Rom. 3:24).

"justified by faith apart from the deeds of the law" (Rom. 3:28).

"By whom also we have access by faith into his *grace*" (Rom. 5:2).

"much more they who receive abundance of *grace*" (Rom. 5:17).

"even so might *grace* reign through righteousness" (Rom. 5:21).

"for ye are not under the law but under *grace* (Rom. 6:14).

"we are not under the law, but under *grace*" (Rom. 6:15).

"ye also are become dead to the law by the body of Christ" (Rom. 7:4).

"For Christ is the *end (telos*=ending, termination, finish) of the law for righteousness to everyone that believeth" (Rom. 10:4).

"We . . . beseech you also that ye receive not the *grace* of God in vain" (2 Cor. 6:1).

"And God is able to make all *grace* abound toward you" (2 Cor. 9:8).

"My *grace* is sufficient for thee" (2 Cor. 12:9).

"not being myself under the law" (1 Cor. 9:20).

"a man is not justified by the works of the law" (Gal. 2:16).

"But if ye be led by the Spirit, ye are not under the law" (Gal. 5:18).

"by *grace* ye are saved" (Eph. 2:5) "through faith" (Eph. 2:8).

"the exceeding riches of his *grace*" (Eph. 2:7).

"Having abolished in his flesh the enmity, even the law of commandments contained in ordinances" (Eph. 2:15).

"But unto every one of us is *given grace*" (Eph. 4:7).

"Be strong in the *grace* that is in Christ Jesus" (2 Tim. 2:1).

"the *grace* of God that bringeth *salvation* . . . to all men" (Titus 2:11).

"being justified by his *grace,* we should be made heirs" (Titus 3:7).

"*Grace* be with you all" (Titus 3:15, Paul's closing "signature").

"For the law made nothing perfect" (Heb. 7:19).

"This is the *true grace* of God in which ye stand" (1 Peter 5:12).

"But *grow in grace,* and in the knowledge of our Lord Jesus Christ" (2 Peter 3:18). We are never told to grow in old Jewish laws!

✿ ✿ ✿

Free from the law, O happy condition,
Jesus hath bled, and there is remission;
Cursed by the law and bruised by the fall,
Christ hath redeemed us once for all.

> Now we are free—there's no condemnation,
> Jesus provides a perfect salvation;
> "Come unto Me," O hear His sweet call,
> Come and He saves us once for all.
> —Philip P. Bliss

* * *

Holding Fast to Grace is a delightful book written by Dr. Roy L. Aldrich while president of the Detroit, Michigan, Bible College. The author's Introduction summarizes the main thrust of the book.

> The most persistent and widespread and deadly error of all Bible history is legalism. The natural mind has an affinity for legalism and corresponding disaffection for grace. The multitudes prefer to spend their money and labor in a vain attempt to merit what God declares can be secured "without money and without price" (Isa. 55:1, 2).
> The believer, saved through grace, is God's masterwork (Eph. 2:1–10).
> But those who are saved by grace are not automatically delivered from legalism. The old nature, with its affinity for a merit system, still remains. The Galatian Christians were saved by grace but later entangled in dangerous forms of Mosaic legalism. "Are ye so foolish? having begun in the Spirit, are ye now made perfect by the flesh" (Gal. 3:3).
> We shall show that the believer is free from every aspect of the law of Moses including the Ten Commandments. Some will consider this such rank heresy that they will read no further. However, if the language of the New Testament is to be taken at its face value, such a conclusion is not only inevitable but it is the only position that avoids contradictions and inconsistencies.

Dr. Aldrich shows clearly that to magnify New Testament grace over Old Testament law is NOT to promote antinomianism or lawlessness. To show that we are now under a far better New Testament law, the author quotes from many of the world's finest Christians. Among them are Evan Hopkins, Howard Taylor, Hannah W. Smith, Oswald J. Sanders, Brother Lawrence, Lewis Sperry Chafer, Charles G. Finney, F. B. Meyer, Theodore Monod, D. W. Whittle, Ruth Paxson, Elizabeth Elliott, A. W. Tozer, Norman B. Harrison, Steven Barabas, and Donald G. Barnhouse. These represent many denominations, as could be expected. Many others could be named.

Thousands of saintly men and women like the above have taught us—

> Marvelous grace of our loving Lord,
> Grace that exceeds our sin and our guilt. . .

When do genuine Christians feel closest to the Lord, more sure of the Spirit's indwelling, and most grateful for God's grace? When does 1 John 3:24 seem most precious—"And by this we know that he (Christ) abideth in us, by the Spirit whom he hath given us." Is it not when we hear or sing a song like—

> Amazing Grace! how sweet the sound
> That saved a wretch like me!
> I once was lost, but now am found,
> Was blind, but now I see.
>
> 'Twas grace that taught my heart to fear,
> And grace my fears relieved;
> How precious did that grace appear
> The hour I first believed.
>   —John Newton

40

HOW TO DEFEAT
ARMSTRONGISM

WE HAVE PRAYED much that God would help us write so as to be of utmost help to all readers, including those now entangled by Armstrongism.

Therefore we may be frank in saying that a careful use of this book should be helpful in meeting and answering most of the cults.

Satan has tried to hinder this writing. An indescribable, ominous feeling of obstruction comes, such as in previous years when preparing a sermon on the devil and his deceptive work. Satan does not want himself and his work exposed. The Apostle Paul said Satan hindered him (1 Thes. 2:18). Assuredly, Satan will do his best to hinder the reading of this work, but we believe that God has supreme power.

As gardeners and farmers defeat weeds by careful planning and much hard work, so we believe individuals and churches can defeat Satan's cults by earnest work and much hard study of the Bible.

For cultists and their leaders are neither omnipotent nor infallible. "The founders of the more popular cults are by no means all finished scholars; too often they are bunglers who stumble upon an idea, and afterward bolster it with pickings from many fields" (J. K. Van Baalen, in *The Chaos of Cults,* p. 11. Eerdmans).

But our churches had better wake up and go to work! If a

farmer is not skilled in weed control, the weeds will win. Beautiful farms by the thousands demonstrate that weeds need *not* win. Just so, many healthy churches are now thriving because they are so busy doing good work that the weeds of evil doctrine have little chance to grow.

For instance, the First Presbyterian Church of Hollywood, California, puts each of its elders and deacons through a three-year course in church history and doctrine. And this course is demanding; it is not easy.

"A minister who will sit down and study, and afterward will stand up and teach, will do more for his people than one who runs from pillar to post and is present at a ceaseless round of 'church activities.'" (J. K. Van Baalen, *ibid.*, 386).

Modern cultists are formidable foes. They are keen about their peculiar beliefs. They are hostile as the devil toward evangelical Christians. They will resent anyone who tries to correct them, and they know the weaknesses in our average churches. Many cultists sacrifice far more for their "faith" than most of our church members do. And they feel so superior; they think they have something newer and better than the rest of us, and many are trained to be clever propagandists. With demon possession growing, one would expect to find Satanic influence in most cults.

The usual plan of most cultists is to cite some few Bible texts for their views, with a "so there" attitude. But in each case of difference, such texts can be refuted by a skilled pastor or lay-man who can cite *more relevant* texts which modify or cancel the peculiar slant of heretics.

"No prophecy of the Scripture is of any private interpretation" (2 Peter 1:20). This means that any one verse must be understood in the light of other Bible verses which bear on the same subject. It also means that no one person—as a cult leader—has a right to impose any meaning he likes on a verse of Scripture.

Christ taught us this big lesson in His dialogue with Satan (Matt. 4:1–11). Satan quoted from Psalm 91 but Jesus countered with a bigger text in Deuteronomy 6. A bigger text is one that states a constant law or principle, in contrast to smaller texts which may apply only to certain few people, places, times or conditions.

We can defeat the cults by working hard at ten rules.

1. We must know our Bibles well—thoroughly. Get a bird's-eye view of it as a whole. Study it with a good Bible hand book, or "Introduction" or a brief commentary. Fix firmly in mind that the Bible is in two main parts. The Old Testament is for the past; the New is for the present and the future. Do not sew old cloth on a new garment; do not mix Jewish legalism with Christian grace.

The transition period between the old and new covenants presents some problems. Do not expect a precise time or verse to divide them cleanly. We read in Luke 16:16 that "the law and the prophets were until John (the Baptist)" and that must be when the transition began. But we also read that years later, Paul and Peter disputed about certain old Jewish laws (Gal. 2:1-4). We should also expect the Jewish sabbaths to be observed for a time, until the far greater meaning of Christ's resurrection made the First Day to be observed properly as the Lord's Day.

2. We must try to read verses analytically. If we read carelessly we could miss the point in 2 Corinthians 3:6-17. Notice the particular law "done away" and "abolished" is identified by the phrase "engraved in stones" and by the added fact that Moses' face shone when the law was given. This *has to* mean the Ten Commandments, for no other laws are thus identified. We now have higher and better laws in the New Testament. Because of "the dispensation of the grace of God" in which we now live, we obey Him out of sheer gratitude instead of for fear of breaking old Jewish laws.

3. Use a good concordance. Notice that one word may have several meanings, depending on the context. Thus the word "law" in Exodus will be different from "law" in First John.

4. Notice what Christ has done for us *now*. As He gave instant salvation to the repentant thief on the cross, so He gives immediate salvation to ALL who now confess their sins, and who receive Him sincerely as their Lord and Savior. "It is finished," He said on the cross, meaning His work of redemption. "When He had by himself purged our sins" (Heb. 1:3) means ALL our sins. He saves us before and without baptism—which should follow as a matter of obedience. And he wants us in evangelical churches where faithful pastors lead us into dedicated service for Him.

In Christ's parables of the kingdom of heaven (Matt. 13), He warns us of dangers such as false cults, proselyters and wolves in sheep's clothing. Peter, Paul and Jude gave us many similar warnings.

We should emphasize the *leadership* of Christ, and His *Cross*. Sects and cults are weak on these vital points.

More, Christ will come back for us, perhaps very soon. Then our trials and failures and weaknesses will all be over. Thank God for that.

5. The Holy Spirit, if we listen, will guide us into all truth. For He IS a Person; He is omnipotent and omnipresent and omniscient. He is the Spirit of Christ, and He upholds the Word of God. Beware of false prophets who may *say* they obey the Spirit, but how can they when they deny His Personality?

The Holy Spirit is powerful enough to win for us, against all foes.

6. Speak up for the Bible at every proper opening. In Sunday School classes, in homes, in visits, in conversations and in letters —lend your voice and influence on the side of God's revealed word.

7. Try to promote sound doctrinal teachings and preaching in churches. Pray for, and counsel with, the pastor as to promoting true doctrine in sermons, books, magazines, radio, television and in home devotions. The Sunday School teachers and literature must be chosen carefully. Also, get everyone so busy in Great Commission evangelism that no time will be left over for the empty follies and perils of cultists.

8. Organize a series of studies in Sunday School, Sunday evenings, or in prayer meetings. Have five, ten, or thirteen sessions with a qualified leader, and with books for every person in the group. (Do not bury this book in a church library only!) A class on the Menace of Armstrongism will inform members about many important Bible doctrines. It will also help each person to deal intelligently with possible victims of cults.

9. Urge friends and relatives to secure copies of books like this; urge them to read and then discuss matters of interest after reading.

10. Give, lend, or sell to any friend or relative who may show some interest in Armstrongism. A stitch in time saves nine. A book in time may save nine people for Christ and His (your)

church. Some member of your church could perform a valuable service by promoting such a book as this to his friends and neighbors. This is one way to let one's light shine for the glory of God and for the welfare of His church.

"The GRACE of our Lord Jesus Christ be with your spirit."

BIBLIOGRAPHY

Adair, J. R. and Miller, Ted, WE FOUND OUR WAY OUT. Grand Rapids: Baker Book House, Fifth Printing, 1968.

Aldrich, Roy L., HOLDING FAST TO GRACE. Findlay, Ohio: Dunham Publishing Company, n.d.

BIBLIOTHECA SACRA. Dallas, Texas: Dallas Thelogical Seminary

Bogard, Ben M., HERESIES EXPOSED. Texarkana, Texas: Baptist Sunday School Committee, n.d.

Campbell, Roger F., H. W. ARMSTRONG—MR. CONFUSION. Lincoln Nb.: Back to the Bible Broadcast, 1969

Canright, D. M. SEVENTH DAY ADVENTISM RENOUNCED. New York: Revell, 1914.

Chambers, THE PLAIN TRUTH ABOUT ARMSTRONGISM. Baker Book House, 1972.

Clark, George W., NOTES ON MARK. Philadelphia: American Baptist Publication Society, 1872

Dahlin, John E., "Delusions on a Rampage" in THE DISCERNER. Minneapolis: Jan.-March, 1962.

Dana & Mantey, MANUAL GRAMMAR OF THE GREEK NEW TESTAMENT. New York: Macmillan, 23rd Printing, 1958.

DeHaan, M. R., IS THE BELIEVER UNDER LAW? Grand Rapids: Radio Bible Class, 1970

DeHaan, Richard W., WHO CHANGED THE SABBATH? Radio Bible Class, 1697.

DeLoach, Charles F., THE ARMSTRONG ERROR. Plainfield, N. J.: Logos International, 1971.

Edersheim, Alfred, THE LIFE AND TIMES OF JESUS THE MESSIAH. Grand Rapids: Eerdmans, 1956.

ENCYCLOPEDIA BRITANNICA.

Grant, Robert G., THE PLAIN TRUTH ABOUT THE ARMSTRONG CULT. Second Edition.

Irvine, A. C., HERESIES EXPOSED. Chicago: Moody Press, 7th Ed., 1930.

Kirban, Salem, DOCTRINES OF DEVILS, No. 1: ARMSTRONG'S CHURCH OF GOD

———— THE PLAIN TRUTH ABOUT THE PLAIN TRUTH. Huntington Valley, Pa., 1970.

Lowe, Harry W., RADIO CHURCH OF GOD. Mt. View, Cal: Pacific Press Pub. Co. 1970.

MARSON REPORT CONCERNING H. W. ARMSTRONG, 1970.

Martin, Walter R., THE KINGDOM OF THE CULTS. Minneapolis: Bethany Fellowship. Revised Edition, 1968.

McClain, Alva J., LAW AND GRACE. Chicago: Moody Press, 1967.

Ray, R. L., APOSTLES OF DISCORD. Boston: Beacon Press, 1953.

Rice, John R., FALSE DOCTRINES ANSWERED. Murfreesboro, Tenn.: Sword of the Lord Publishers, 1970.

Robertson, A. T., WORD PICTURES IN THE NEW TESTAMENT, six volumes. New York: Harpers, 1953.

Smith, Noel, H. W. ARMSTRONG AND HIS WORLD TO-MORROW, 7th Printing. Springfield, Mo.: Baptist Bible Tribune, 1964.

Van Baalen, J. K., THE CHAOS OF CULTS. Grand Rapids: Eerdmans, 3rd Ed., 1960.

ADDENDA

Why do many people leave Armstrong, after having been his loyal followers? Charles F. DeLoach was a member of the so-called "Worldwide Church of God" but he left it when he was converted to simple faith in Christ. Since then he has written a 117-page book, *The Armstrong Error*. This book exposes Armstrongism which he calls "a masterpiece of Satanic deceit."

* * *

Richard A. Marson wrote a 175-page book—"an exhaustive analysis of Mr. Armstrong's version of the Anglo-Israelite Theory." Mr. Marson was a former member of Armstrong's church—until he investigated it.

* * *

Mr. and Mrs. Leyendecker were "hooked" by Armstrong's propaganda, but "the conflicts within grew rather than subsided." They asked a pastor to help them, and he emphasized simple faith in Christ. Later: "We are grateful to God that he guided us out of the errors of Armstrongism into the truth of Christ and his salvation. It was such a relief to find that all the demands of God's law were fulfilled in Jesus Christ, and our hearts' demands for peace and assurance are also fulfilled in Him." (From, *We Found Our Way Out*, Baker Book House.)

* * *

Armstrongism robs its victims of the purely *Christian* joys of Christmas, Easter and all Sundays—those joys totally separate from any paganism. Who else is against Christmas? Ebenezer Scrooge with his "Bah! Christmas humbug!" And Herod who had all boy babies under two in Bethlehem killed; he would agree with Armstrong's saying "The day of death is better than the day of one's birth." Against Christmas also: atheists, infidels, Jews, Moslems, Buddhists, Shintoists and pagans.

* * *

"Should Christians Observe the Feast Days of Leviticus 23?" The answer is a decisive "NO" as given in the November, 1972, *Bible Advocate* (for which Herbert W. Armstrong formerly wrote, and once endorsed). Items—

1. Those feasts were given to the *nation* of Israel, and to no one else.

2. There is no hint that Israel observed them before leaving Egypt.

3. Those feasts were to be observed in Jerusalem only (2 Chron. 33:7).

4. Those feasts were temporary in nature (Isa. 1:13, 14; Hosea 2:11).

5. During Christ's time the Jews observed them, but Christ did not.

6. Neither John the Baptist nor Jesus commanded feasts. They preached the kingdom which "is not meat and drink" (Rom. 14:17). "The law and the prophets were *until John*" (Luke 16:16; Matt. 11:13; Mark 1:1; Acts 10:37; 13:24).

7. Christ did not enforce the Mosaic law in John 8:3-11. "Neither do I condemn thee; go and sin no more." The Mosaic law demanded stoning to death. Christ's way is "better" than Moses' (Heb. 7:19, 22; 8:6, 13; 9:23).

8. Jesus taught a change in worship and place of worship (John 4:21-24), meaning an end of feasts and feast days.

9. Christ endorsed the eternal moral laws of God, not Moses' temporary laws.

10. Christ's death on the cross fulfilled the Passover types; those keeping the passovers now insult Christ by implying His death was not enough.

* * *

The Bible tells us to "avoid foolish questions, and genealogies, and contentions, and strivings about the law; for they are unprofitable and vain" (Titus 3:9). But H. W. Armstrong insists that he can trace his own genealogy all the way back to Adam! And he harps incessantly on the old Jewish laws, contrary to the entire book of Galatians.

Obey the Old Testament laws, especially the sabbaths and feast days, says Armstrong—or it is the lake of fire. Like a bank robber pointing his gun at a teller who is forced to hand over the bank's money to the crook. So the Armstrongs win members by scare tactics—and with lies. When they twist "habitations" in Exodus 35:3 to mean foundries—as they do—they win people by outright falsehoods.

Why are Armstrong's meetings secret? No meeting allowed without an Armstrong "minister" present? No outsiders invited? "There shall be false teachers among you, who secretly shall bring in destructive heresies, even denying the Lord that bought them" (2 Peter 2:1).

Mrs. C. L. G. of Dallas, Texas: "For several years I listened to Armstrong . . . But one night I heard him say it was impossible for Jesus to be the Son of God. I turned him off right then, and have never listened to him again. I also wrote and told him not to send his *Plain Truth* magazine any more." (From the January, 1973, *Moody Monthly.)*

* * *

Mr. Armstrong uses "The Eternal" instead of Lord, even in his songs which are pitifully devoid of the Christian gospel Why? The name "Lord" is found over 6,000 times in the Old Testament. It means Master, or Ruler. Judas never addressed Christ as Lord, the name used about 600 times in the New Testament. *No verse* in the Bible calls God "The Eternal." Nearest is "The Eternal God" (Deut. 33:27). See also 1 Cor. 12:3 on this issue.

* * *

One of Armstrong's ministers referred to "the heathen" who have Sunday Schools. These "heathen" include millions of Bible-loving Christians! So the Armstrongs join in Satan's work as "the accuser of our brethren" (Rev. 12:10). They call 99% of Christians in words that are "most venomous and vitriolic and wildly censorious."

Garner Ted Armstrong's article, "What Is a Real Christian?" denounces all non-Armstrongites as disobedient, ignorant, misinformed and misled. Only his own select group really understand the Bible! His article has about 85 mistakes, plus haughty hateful words against Christian people.

H. W. Armstrong, in his tract on baptism, page 5: "The true gospel . . . was not primarily about Himself (Christ) . . ." He said the "true" gospel was not about the person of Christ; it was the good news of the government of God. How terribly, awfully wrong he is; see 1 Cor. 15:1-4. What a shame to downgrade Christ, as the Armstrongs have done for so long.

* * *

Repeatedly the Armstrong literature has said they had only

two 19-year periods to preach their "true" gospel which they started Jan. 7, 1934. But after this prophetic date-setting expired Jan. 7, 1972, they have made many excuses. They "never set dates" they said! But they lie. Their book, *"1975 in Prophecy"* is a date-setting book by its very title. This book has horrible pictures, perhaps meant to frighten people. It predicted a devastating drought by 1975, or "probably between 1965 and 1972!" And that was to mark "the beginning of the great tribulation," he said. "When a prophet speaks . . . if the thing follow not, nor come to pass, that is the thing which *the Lord hath not spoken,* but the prophet hath spoken it presumptuously; *thou shalt not be afraid of him"* (Deut. 18:22).

❊ ❊ ❊

"Monopoly" is a favorite game with many. The Armstrongs play it seriously; they claim to have a monopoly on knowledge of prophecy and of the "true" gospel. Their "monopoly" brings them millions every month. They entice people to play with them by offering "free literature." Gamblers entice amateurs by letting them win some early games, but later—?

❊ ❊ ❊

"Stand fast, therefore, in the liberty with which Christ hath made us free, and be not entangled again with the yoke of bondage" (Gal. 5:1).

X X X

❊ ❊ ❊

"I am excited about your manuscript on Armstrongism. This is the most thorough treatise that I have seen on this subject. God has given you this text . . . I see tremendous possibilities for this good study."

—The late S. Ray Sadler